Minnesota's Bounty

To Suez!
I've learned
so Much!
Much! Love!
Beth!

Minnesota's Bounty

The Farmers Market Cookbook

Beth Dooley

Photographs by Mette Nielsen

University of Minnesota Press
Minneapolis / London

Published by the University of Minnesota Press
111 Third Avenue South, Suite 290
Minneapolis, MN 55401-2520
http://www.upress.umn.edu

Book design by Brian Donahue / bedesign, inc.

ISBN 978-0-8166-7315-5 (pb)
A Cataloging-in-Publication record is available from the Library of Congress.

Printed in China on acid-free paper

The University of Minnesota is an equal-opportunity educator and employer.

20 19 18 17 16 15 14 13   10 9 8 7 6 5 4 3 2 1

Contents

Vegetables

Meat and Fish

Market Essentials

Farmers Market Menus *266*

Mhonpaj Lee of Mhonpaj's Garden is one of the region's first Hmong farmers to use organic practices.

Introduction

Hit the Market Forget the List

At 6:00 a.m. on a brilliant October morning twenty years ago, I arrived at the St. Paul Farmers Market in search of local apples. Swept into a whirlwind of colors and aromas—brilliant orange squash, vibrant green beans, glossy eggplant, crimson crab apples, and the spicy bouquet of hot and sweet peppers—I fell in love; I've come back each week ever since. What I've found here is far more than the makings of applesauce and a week's groceries. The tables, heaped with the season's bounty, are living calendars. Even in the dead of winter, I gather wildflower honey, maple syrup, cheese, eggs, meats, poultry, game, bread, root vegetables, flour, and grains. Every farmers market is a glorious Mardi Gras that engages our senses and lifts our spirits. Waiting in line for coffee, I chat with other enthusiasts and share recipes, stories, and memories of meals past.

Through conversations with growers, I've learned more about my food than I have ever encountered in a classroom or through books. I've come to understand how the methods used to produce vegetables and apples or make cheese affect their flavor and nutrition and our economy, water, and land. Local market farmers rely on sustainable practices: rotating crops that restore nutrients to the soil and employing pest-eating critters in lieu of the chemicals that pollute groundwater and air. Lamb, pork, beef, buffalo, chicken, dairy, and egg farmers do not use antibiotics or hormones, and their animals range free.

Independent and self-reliant, these farmers must manage the forces of nature as well as local and international politics. "Ask me about the farm bill, commodity price supports, shallow-loss crop insurance, for big corn and soy growers," says Gene Thomas

St. Paul Farmers Market is the country's oldest continuous retail farmers market. As early as 1852, St. Paul city founders wrote, "It is the responsibility of the City to provide a farmers market to its people." Its charter requires that all vendors grow or produce their food within the foodshed.

PHOTOGRAPH BY CHARLES ALFRED ZIMMERMAN. COURTESY OF THE MINNESOTA HISTORICAL SOCIETY.

Kordner, in his St. Paul vegetable stall, "and you'll understand what we're up against. Farming is not merely a business, it's a life."

If we are what we eat, then regular trips to the farmers markets help us learn not just *who* but *where* we are, in time and place. When I exchange money with the farmer whose potatoes resemble his earth-stained hands, I'm reminded that this is as close as I will ever get to planting, weeding, and harvesting the stuff myself. These direct transactions between farmer and cook, ancient as civilization, connect the city to the country and us to the earth.

The story of the St. Paul Farmers Market, the oldest continuous retail farmers market in the country, and the Minneapolis Farmers Market, once the country's largest produce wholesale market, is repeated throughout the Northern Heartland today. Despite our short growing season and intense climate, farmers markets are booming. The past ten years have seen a 50 percent spike in the number of markets and their sales of local food. They are the gathering place for those of us concerned about a secure local food system, one that provides fresh, delicious, nutritious, chemical-free food to everyone; one that protects our natural resources and ensures a fair income for producers. There is nothing precious, expensive, or exclusive here. Farmers markets are good for the cooks, good for the growers, good for us all.

Tale of Two Markets

The farmers markets of St. Paul and Minneapolis are among the country's oldest continuous markets. Today, both are run by their growers associations. The history of these two powerful markets tells the story of our region's food.

The St. Paul Farmers Market

Located in historic Lowertown, the St. Paul Farmers Market was founded as an essential component of the city. As early as 1852, the founders wrote, "It is the responsibility of the City to provide a farmers market to its people." What visionaries these forefathers were. Today, even some of the country's most successful and highly acclaimed markets do not have guaranteed long-term leases, thus their continued security is a concern.

The St. Paul Farmers Market was first housed in a two-story brick market house designed by architect Abraham Radcliffe. Erected at Seventh and Wabasha Streets, it sported a clock tower, large vaulted windows, and storefronts that sparked trade downtown. In those early years, St. Paul was a frontier town, ringed by log cabins connected by dirt streets. Steamboat traffic clogged the Mississippi, and the city was a major port for lumber and wheat.

The market house provided St. Paul residents with seasonal produce, cheese, eggs, dairy, and flour as well as cakes and candles all year long. The second floor housed the city's library until 1915, when a cauldron of candy in a confectionary shop bubbled over, smothered the flame of a gas stove, and caused a devastating explosion. The current location of the St. Paul Farmers Market, at Fifth and Wall Streets, is not far from the original site, and its physical structure is reminiscent of the early market's outdoor stalls protected by a corrugated roof.

Much of what we see today began in the 1970s when Dick Broeker, a city planner, and George Latimer, St. Paul's mayor at the time, set the city on a mission to restore historic buildings and reconnect downtown to the river. Thanks to their work, the St. Paul Farmers Market is a key player in today's local food movement. It is governed by a growers association, which each vendor must join, that establishes the guidelines, employs the market manager, and funds the market's administrative costs. Its bylaws require that its vendors must supply their own products, grown or made on their own properties in Minnesota or Wisconsin. Resale is not allowed.

The St. Paul Farmers Market has long served as the venue for the waves of immigrants to this harsh yet promising land. Newly settled Mexican, Hmong, Somali, and Cambodian market vendors have assimilated to our culture and introduced us to theirs. Through shopping at the market, I've learned how to use bitter melon and the tiny red chilies sometimes called "chicken leg horn" peppers by lingering to chat with market family teenagers fluent in two or more languages. The income earned from these intrepid entrepreneurs has funded college educations, restaurants, and food businesses over the years.

Just across the street, the award-winning Heartland Restaurant and Farm Market Direct showcase chef-owner Lenny Russo's passion for and panache with local foods. Here you'll find house-made prosciutto (crafted from local pork) and artisanal oils and vinegars to dress your farmers market goods as well as a great cup of coffee and a pastry to start the day.

The Minneapolis Farmers Market

Established in 1937 as a wholesale market, the Minneapolis Farmers Market was seeded in 1876 when, on the corner of First Street and Hennepin Avenue, the Minneapolis Fruit and Vegetable Market supplied the city with fresh food. It moved to Third Avenue North and Sixth and Seventh Streets and drew over 400 vendors who supplied the produce

The Minneapolis Farmers Market, founded in 1876 as the Minneapolis Fruit and Vegetable Market, was once the country's largest produce wholesale market and supplied the city with fresh food. It remains one of the country's largest farmers markets today.
PHOTOGRAPH BY JACOBY. COURTESY OF THE MINNESOTA HISTORICAL SOCIETY.

warehouses and wholesale outlets that made Minneapolis one of the top produce distribution centers in the United States until the early 1990s.

Through the city's history, the market has evolved along with our food system. In the mid-1960s, as supermarkets began purchasing produce directly from growers and packers, wholesalers began opening up sales to smaller accounts and individual shoppers who, enticed by variety and price, made the Minneapolis Farmers Market a good source for retail sales.

Coincidentally, smaller farmers and producers sought stalls at the Minneapolis Farmers Market where they could sell directly to shoppers and capture a fair price for their food. Today the Minneapolis

Farmers Market supports about 230 vendors in its 170 stalls and has a satellite market on Nicollet Mall.

Perhaps the key difference between the St. Paul and Minneapolis farmers markets is the focus on local. Because Minneapolis's market originated as a wholesale market, many of the resale vendors are grandfathered in, but as they retire, local growers and processors are taking their places. Every vendor is required to display a sign that states whether he or she is a local grower, producer, or manufacturer or a licensed reseller.

Farmers at Market

"On market day, we're up around 4:00 a.m. to finish the harvest and load the truck," says Laura Frerichs, who, with her husband and

business partner, Adam Cullip, runs Loon Organics (Hutchinson, Minnesota). Frerichs, a Mill City Market grower, adds, "We have loyal customers who come early each Saturday and buy their week's produce from our farm. It gives us a chance to talk to them and learn their preferences. We've formed wonderful friendships over the years." Frerichs and Cullip's sales have doubled since they joined the market when it first opened six years ago.

But, given the short season and challenging climate, most farms rely on more than one outlet. "Seventy-five percent of our sales are through community supported agriculture, aka CSA," notes Frerichs. In this arrangement, the farmer receives an advance payment for a season's worth of vegetables that are distributed weekly. Mill City Farmers Market is a CSA pickup location for Loon Organics. "Some of our CSA members buy more vegetables from us when they pick up their shares," Frerichs adds.

Too Many Markets?

Are there too many markets? Currently, St. Paul hosts more than a dozen satellite markets in residential neighborhoods. Each of the farmers markets in Minneapolis is independent. Some vendors feel they must participate in several markets to gross what they used to make at one big market. There is concern that these farmers are being spread thin. But for newer growers who are squeezed out of the large markets for lack of space or because of cost, the new, smaller markets provide a service to both farmers and shoppers.

The issue is a lack of coordination among farmers markets and the farmers themselves, notes David Nicholson, a former Kingfield Farmers Market manager and a consultant. "There's no means to make considered decisions about where new markets appear," he notes. "Many will argue that the market should decide which farmers markets thrive.

But that view doesn't account for the fact that vendors, who have the most skin in the game, have the least control over the placement and number of markets in an area. They are the big losers when marketplace competition or poor management or location security causes a farmers market to fail."

Small producers have found that farmers markets provide a safe venue for launching their businesses and testing new products. Take as an example Cedar Summit Farm, which relied on the St. Paul Farmers Market as a primary outlet for selling milk in its early years. At the market, members of the Minar family talked directly with their customers, explained the benefits of grass-fed dairy cows, offered samples of their delicious milk, and developed a loyal following of shoppers who continued to buy Cedar Summit milk when it was made available in co-ops.

Mary Falk of LoveTree Farmstead Cheese and Steven Read of Shepherd's Way Farms rely on the farmers markets for a large share of their sales. Though both companies sell some of their cheese through other outlets, they reserve some of their special, limited-quantity cheeses for the loyal farmers and market shoppers who can't find them anywhere else. Mhonpaj's Garden, the area's first certified organic Hmong farm, sells much of its produce at the Mill City Farmers Market and the St. Paul Farmers Market and attracts people to the classes and seminars it gives about Hmong herbs.

Minnesota Markets Today

Along with its main market site in downtown St. Paul, the St. Paul Farmers Market holds smaller satellite markets around the city and in the surrounding suburbs. In addition to the big Minneapolis Farmers Market, Minneapolis hosts the Mill City Farmers Market, one of the prettiest markets in the country, along the banks of the Mississippi River. Smaller markets continue to spring up in Minneapolis neighborhoods: Kingfield, Fulton, Midtown, Linden Hills. All markets focus on education and community, and some offer cooking and nutrition classes, demonstrations, and music. Their Web sites profile their farmers and local foods as well as provide recipes and useful kitchen information.

No doubt, the best farmers market is the one closest to your home. As of this writing, there are at least 146 farmers markets throughout Minnesota; each one is as unique as the farmers and community it serves. Loyalties between farmer and shopper—cultivated week to week, month to month, year to year—make opening day something of a homecoming for growers and cooks. Many markets do function year-round on a limited basis, featuring meat, poultry, game, eggs, fish, cheese, storage crops, pickles, preserves, jams, jellies, and artisanal crafts.

The Web site for the Minnesota Farmers Market Association, www.mfma.org, is a directory of the state's markets with links to individual market Web sites. A glance at this sampling of our markets gives a sense of the variety and individuality of markets across the state:

- **Alexandria Farmers Market:** Spread out at Big Ole Central Park, the town green, this is a great market to stop at before heading to camp in the North Woods.
- **Duluth Farmers Market:** Founded in 1911, the Duluth Farmers Market, housed in a long, low red building set into the hillside, overlooks Lake Superior. The orchards of nearby Bayfield are well represented, so you will find a wealth of berries, cherries, apples, pears, and apricots. If you are attending one of Duluth's summer festivals, the market is a must.
- **Ely Farmers Market:** Ely boasts the shortest growing season in the state, but you'll still find fresh produce, meat, and eggs at its market. If you are heading to

the Boundary Waters, this is a good place to pick up artisanal jerky.
- **Fulton Farmers Market** (Saturdays), **Kingfield Farmers Market** (Sundays), and **Linden Hills Farmers Market** (Sundays): Smaller than the bigger downtown markets, these neighborhood-run Minneapolis farmers markets have a slower, grassroots pace.
- **Grand Marais Farmers Market:** A must for anyone hitting the Gunflint Trail. A tiny gem, located right off Lake Superior, the market showcases fresh and smoked fish, honey, maple syrup, fresh dairy, and produce.
- **Mentor Farmers Market:** The farmers spread out in the city park to sell a range of Amish baskets, flowers, pickles, and preserves as well as native wild rice, elk, eggs, and lamb.
- **Nisswa Farmers Market:** Snuggled among the pine trees next to the Paul Bunyan trail, this is a good market for those heading up north to the lake for the weekend. Native wild rice and quilts are included among the produce, meat, and eggs.
- **Rochester Downtown Farmers Market:** Located in the heart of the Driftless Area, the Rochester region's river bluffs have mild microclimates perfect for growing a wide range of berries, apples, pears, and exotic heirloom crops. The market also offers lefse, artisanal fruit vinegars, and stone-ground flour.
- **St. Paul satellite markets:** Along with the downtown St. Paul Farmers Market, there are more than a dozen satellite markets serving neighborhoods in suburban locations near St. Paul. Smaller farms may begin at a satellite as a way to later become a market vendor, moving higher on the waiting list as farmers rotate off from the larger markets.
- **Winona Farmers Market:** Set in the heart of town on Main Street, the Winona

market surprises with fresh ginger, shiitake mushrooms, hops, and heirloom crops you won't find in the northern parts of the state.

Organic/Local/Sustainable

Perhaps the biggest benefit of shopping at a farmers market is meeting the producers and learning about the difference between small local and organic farms and large-scale conventional operations. Organic farmers use environmentally sound practices that address the economic, philosophical, political, and social challenges caused by the harmful practices of large-scale farms. These methods reflect a philosophy rather than a set of rigid requirements. These farmers use natural methods to improve soil productivity and water quality. They avoid pesticides and fertilizers, manage healthy animals without the use of antibiotics and hormones, and support themselves and their workers with fair pay and safe working conditions.

In many cases, the smallest farmers are not certified organic, but don't let that stop you from purchasing their food. Ask them about their practices; they are required to reveal whether they use sprays, fertilizers, or chemicals. Some will argue that the cost of organic certification is prohibitive and the paperwork is overwhelming and unnecessary. Currently, organic farmers shoulder the burden of certification with little help from the government. Yet their work benefits our environment and provides us with healthy ingredients. Our current farm bill, with its commodity price supports and shallow-loss insurance program, commits our tax dollars to support corn, wheat, cotton, and soy crops that require petroleum-based fertilizers and pesticides. Such chemicals create the very environmental and health problems that our tax dollars are also directed to clean up. In short, shopping at farmers markets supports those using sustainable practices.

How to Use This Book

I don't like recipes. Period.

This may seem odd coming from a cookbook author. But the truth is that a recipe is really no more than a guide. No one, except you, really knows how ripe those tomatoes you just bought are, or the size of your frying pan, or how quirky your oven is. Recipes are meant to guide, not dictate. So just let what is in season, what looks the best, and your own appetite be the factors that help you decide what to eat.

The farmers are your best resources for information, and most are enthusiastic cooks. Many farmers and producers have brochures and recipes to share. I credit much of what I know about food storage, handling, and preparation to casual conversations with farmers, butchers, and cheesemakers.

My approach to the market? I like to grab a cup of coffee and stroll the aisles, checking out the different market stalls to get a sense of where I'd like to focus. Then I begin to buy an assortment of vegetables, fruit, cheese, eggs, meat, and honey. Often I will be able to stock up on enough fresh food to last our family (ranging from three to five, plus assorted friends) well into the week.

I don't have any particular recipes in mind when I shop, but I do imagine how these foods will work together into a meal: fat spears of asparagus inspire quiche with good bacon, farm eggs, and soft sheep cheese; tomatoes mean gazpacho, so I'll add cucumbers, peppers, and onions to my basket. Walking and talking and listening to market chatter, I am energized by all the possible future meals ahead.

This book is an encyclopedia of Northern Heartland foods. The idea is to go to the market, buy what looks best and what you're hungry for, then go home and cook.

Farmers markets offer much more than the makings of a good dinner.

To Market, to Market: What to Expect

Shopping at a farmers market is far different from going to a store. Allow yourself time to become immersed in the experience.

1. **Slow down.** Take in the colors and textures and smells – like fresh coffee, roasting peppers, grilling sausages, damp earth.

2. **Come with a basket or a bag.** Many growers sell bundles of vegetables and pints of fruit but do not supply big, brown grocery bags.

3. **Forget the shopping list.** Let the season inspire your decisions. Look to discover what has just come in; decide what to do with it once you're home.

4. **If you don't recognize a vegetable or fruit, ask the growers:** they love to share what they know.

5. **Bring cash.** Some farmers accept checks, but few take cards.

6. **Taste!** Take the samples that are offered – you don't have to buy. This is a great opportunity to try new foods and start a conversation.

7. **Leave the dog at home.** Most markets ban dogs and all other animals for a variety of health and safety reasons.

8. **Bring the kids.** They will learn a lot about where and how their food is grown, and they will taste some healthy treats.

Fruit

Every apple tells a story.

—GRETCHEN PERBIX, Sweetland Orchard (Webster, Minnesota)

Apples

Farmers markets are showcases for heirloom varieties. Of the fifteen thousand different kinds of apples grown in our country up until the 1950s, a mere three thousand varieties remain. Eleven different kinds of trees produce 90 percent of all the apples sold in our stores.

Here's what you're likely to find at the farmers markets on any given day.

Bonnie Best: "Best for pie!" claims Gretchen Perbix of Sweetland Orchard, who sells apples, cider, and the best donuts at several Twin Cities markets. It's supersweet, requiring little sugar and barely any cinnamon, and its texture is "pitch perfect," she says.

Chestnut Crabapple: These darling little apples are one-bite wonders. They are pretty cored and baked alongside turkey.

Connell Red and Fireside: These apples resemble each other in flavor, texture, and cooking qualities. They are fine for eating out of hand, plenty juicy and complex tasting, and cook up nicely. They're great pressed for cider.

Cortland: This is an all-around apple for eating, baking, and saucing. It's crisp, citrusy, and plenty sweet.

Haralson: Our favorite apple. It's juicy, tart, and stores well.

Honeycrisp: The new favorite. Juicy, crisp, and sweet-tart, it's the choice for eating out of hand but not for baking.

Honeygold: The champagne of apples. It's crisp and mildly perfumed.

Keepsake: This old-timey, hard, crunchy sweet apple has a light scent of roses. It's terrific in sauce too.

Malinda: The parent of Haralson and Chestnut Crabapple, Malinda is a pretty pale green with blushing shoulders. It's not great for cooking but is delicious fresh.

Northwestern Greening: This classic pie apple is terrific for sauce too. It's an older variety, tart and yielding.

Prairie Spy: An all-around apple with dense, dry flesh that's both tart and sweet.

Regent: Sweet-tart flavor makes this apple a favorite; it keeps beautifully.

Scarlet Surprise: Sometimes called scarlet delight, the pretty pink flesh of this apple is truly a surprise. These make a beautiful applesauce, plenty tart and sweet, and are good for eating out of hand.

Wolf River: Sugary sweet, dense, and satisfying; this is a keeper.

COOK'S NOTE

Store apples in the refrigerator, and use the softer apples first.

1 pound = 3 to 5 apples = 2 to 3 cups cored and sliced, diced, or chopped apples

Quick Ideas

Baked Apples: Remove a one-inch circle of skin around the top of the apple and core it. Fill each cavity with dried cranberries and a little maple syrup. Bake at 350 degrees until soft, about 45 minutes. Serve with a scoop of whipped cream.

Easiest Applesauce: Peel, core, and slice a few apples. Put the slices in a pot with a little cider and a cinnamon stick. Cover, and simmer over low heat until the apples dissolve into sauce, about 45 minutes. The longer the apples cook, the thicker and darker the sauce will get.

To make apple butter, remove the lid and continue cooking, stirring occasionally. When the mixture is truly thick and dark, add sugar. Try about 2 tablespoons of sugar per 8 apples to start, adding more to taste.

Savory Applesauce: Follow the directions for Easiest Applesauce, but use several sprigs of rosemary or sage instead of the cinnamon stick. Serve with pork, game, or chicken.

Apple and Cheddar Crostini: Arrange slices of tart, crisp apple over the crostini (toasted bread) and top with slices of artisanal cheddar cheese. Run under the broiler until the cheese is melted and bubbly. Serve hot.

Apple Mint Salsa

Makes about 1 cup

This lively, fresh salsa adds spark to sweet potato soup. It's also delicious on grilled chicken or served as a complement to local cheeses (especially Shepherd's Way Big Woods Blue).

1 small tart, crisp apple, such as Keepsake or Regent
¼ cup chopped fresh mint
1 small jalapeño, seeded,
  deveined, and finely minced
Sprinkling of sugar
Salt and freshly ground pepper

Toss all of the ingredients together in a bowl and serve right away.

Apple Cranberry Chutney

Makes 10 pints

This spicy winter chutney is wonderful with ham and pork or on top of a soft cheese.

2 cups chopped onion
1 large shallot, chopped
¼ cup shredded ginger
4 cups cider vinegar
1 stick cinnamon
12 cups peeled, cored, and chopped apples
2 cups fresh cranberries
4 cups honey
¼ cup Dijon mustard
2 teaspoons cayenne
1 teaspoon salt
2 pounds dried cranberries or raisins

Prepare a stockpot or canner and jars (see page 51).

Combine the onions, shallot, ginger, and some of the vinegar in a blender and purée. Transfer to a stainless-steel or enameled cast-iron kettle, and add the remaining vinegar and the cinnamon, apples, fresh cranberries, honey, mustard, cayenne, and salt. Bring to a boil, reduce the heat, and simmer until thickened, about 45 minutes. Add the dried cranberries, and cook another 10 minutes.

Ladle the hot liquid into the prepared jars, leaving ½ inch of headspace. Wipe the jar rims, center the lids on the jars, and screw on the bands until they are just finger tight.

Process the jars for 10 minutes in enough boiling water to cover the jars by 1 inch. Turn off the heat, remove the canner lid, and allow the jars to stand in the hot water for 5 minutes before removing them. Cool the jars for at least 12 hours before storing them in a cool, dark place.

Apples in Spiced Wine

Serves 4 to 6

This aromatic, spicy compote makes a stunning complement to roast pork, game, or the holiday turkey. Use firm apples such as Keepsake, Jonathan, or Haralson. For the wine, consider a local varietal. Many of our local wineries are making wonderful Riesling wines that would do nicely here.

1 bottle Riesling
1 cinnamon stick
4 whole cloves
1 tablespoon allspice berries
4 tablespoons honey
3 to 4 firm apples, peeled, cored,
 and quartered

In a large saucepan, combine the wine, cinnamon stick, cloves, allspice, and honey and bring to a boil over high heat. Lower the heat, add the apples, and simmer until the apples are tender, about 5 to 10 minutes.

Remove the apples with a slotted spoon and set them aside. Bring the wine back up to a boil, and cook until the liquid is reduced by half. Let the syrup cool.

Pour the cooled syrup over the apples and refrigerate overnight. Bring to room temperature or warm slightly before serving.

Apple Oat Bundt Cake with Cider Brandy Glaze

Makes a 10-inch Bundt cake

Fragrant with warm spices, this robust cake is delicious served warm or at room temperature. If there are any leftovers, toasted slices are wonderful.

CAKE:

1 cup butter, at room temperature
1 cup brown sugar
¾ cup sugar
1 tablespoon vanilla
4 large eggs
2 cups all-purpose flour
½ cup oatmeal (not instant)
2 teaspoons baking powder
1 teaspoon salt
1 cup plain whole-milk yogurt
3 tart apples, peeled, cored, and finely chopped

GLAZE:

1 cup confectioners' sugar
2 tablespoons apple cider
2 tablespoons butter
2 tablespoon applejack or brandy
1 teaspoon cinnamon

Preheat the oven to 325 degrees. Grease and lightly flour a 12-cup Bundt pan.

In a large bowl, beat the butter until it is creamy and smooth, and then beat in the sugars until light and fluffy, about 5 minutes. Beat in the vanilla. Add the eggs one at a time, beating well after each addition.

In a separate bowl, whisk together the flour, oatmeal, baking powder, and salt.

Stir one-third of the flour mixture into the butter mixture; then stir in one-half of the yogurt. Continue adding the flour and yogurt, alternating, until everything is incorporated. Fold in the apples. Scrape the batter into the prepared pan, and bake until a toothpick inserted in the center comes out clean, about 60 to 70 minutes.

Make the glaze while the cake is baking. Put the confectioners' sugar, cider, butter, apple-jack, and cinnamon in a saucepan set over low heat. Whisk until the ingredients are thoroughly combined. The glaze should be thick but pourable. If it is too thick, thin the glaze with a little cider.

As soon as you remove the cake from the oven, use a sharp knife to poke several holes in the cake. Pour half of the glaze over the cake, and allow it to cool for about 10 minutes. Invert the pan, remove the cake, and let it cool completely on the rack. Transfer the cake to a serving plate and drizzle it with the remaining glaze.

Apricots

Our markets are expanding each year as growers experiment with cold-hardy hybrid apricots, cherries, and plums. Our widely fluctuating temperatures often literally nip the fruit trees' blossoms in the bud. Harcot apricots from Canada are making their way to the markets. Brilliant orange and luscious, they're a little smaller than their California cousins and delicious in desserts and salads.

COOK'S NOTE

Apricots bruise easily, so be careful in packing and bringing them home. They will ripen off the tree. Once ripe, refrigerate them.

1 pound = 8 to 12 apricots = 2 $\frac{1}{2}$ to 3 cups sliced or halved apricots

Quick Ideas

Stuffed Apricots: Cut apricots in half and fill the halves with blue cheese or herbed cream cheese.

Apricot Chicken: When sautéing chicken breasts, toss in some sliced apricots when the chicken is almost done.

Apricot Applesauce: Add sliced, peeled apricots to the pan while the applesauce is cooking. Mash or purée before serving.

Poached Apricots

Serves 4

This simple dessert is delicious topped with whipped cream and a few fresh raspberries.

2 pounds apricots
1 ½ cups Riesling or other sweet white wine
¼ cup sugar
1 cinnamon stick
2 cloves
½ cup fresh raspberries (optional)

Bring a pot of water to a boil, and then dip the apricots in, several at a time, to loosen their skins, about 10 to 15 seconds. Remove the skins.

Cut the apricots in half, and remove the pits. In a medium saucepan, bring the wine, sugar, cinnamon, and cloves to a boil. Cook until the liquid is reduced to a cup, about 10 minutes. Strain out the spices, and pour the liquid over the fruit. Chill. Serve with whipped cream or ice cream, and garnish with raspberries if desired.

Apricots Sautéed in Butter

Serves 4 to 6

This old-fashioned sauce is comfort itself. Serve it over ice cream or pound cake. Cut back on the sugar, and it's a sauce for grilled chicken or lamb.

¼ cup unsalted butter
1 pound apricots, pitted and quartered
2 tablespoons to ¼ cup sugar
2 tablespoons brandy

In a large skillet set over medium-high heat, melt the butter until it foams. When the foam subsides, add the apricots and sprinkle on sugar to taste. Cook the apricots, stirring and turning, until they begin to brown, about 10 minutes.

Add the brandy and cook, stirring gently, until the mixture becomes saucy, about a minute. Serve warm.

Blueberries

"Don't worry about the silvery, dusty coating on blueberries; that's the berry's natural protection," says Tom Galazen of North Wind Organic Farm (Bayfield, Wisconsin). "Do worry about sprays, and don't believe anyone who tells you that blueberries can't be grown organically. They taste even better grown without chemicals."

The blueberries most farmers cultivate are the high-bush variety. Plump and succulent, they are different from their wild low-bush cousins. These freeze nicely, so don't hesitate to stock up.

COOK'S NOTE

Blueberries are interchangeable with huckleberries. They have an affinity for citrus, particularly lemon.

1 pint = 2 cups blueberries

Quick Ideas

Salads: Toss blueberries into green salads and grain salads, and serve them on top of chicken salad.

Breads and Muffins: Add blueberries to just about any sweet muffin or quick bread recipe.

Quick Sautés: Toss blueberries in a chicken or lamb sauté, and season with a little chopped thyme or rosemary.

Blueberry Lemon Ginger Sorbet

Serves 4

This tangy sorbet gets a fiery kick from a crystallized ginger.

1 cup sugar
1 cup water
3 pints fresh blueberries
¼ cup fresh lemon juice
¼ cup finely chopped crystallized ginger

Combine the sugar and water in a medium saucepan, and bring it to a boil. Reduce the heat, and simmer for 5 minutes. When the syrup has cooled, pour it into a blender. Add the blueberries and lemon juice, and blend until smooth.

Strain the mixture through a fine-mesh sieve. Refrigerate the mixture until it is cold, and then stir in the ginger. Freeze the sorbet in an ice-cream machine according to the manufacturer's directions.

Breakfast Blueberry Cobbler

Serves 4 to 6

This dish is perfect for a lazy Sunday at the lake when everyone sleeps in and gets up starved (and is far easier than pancakes to whip up). Cobblers are named for the cobbled look created as the batter rises up to become a golden, buttery crust.

3 cups blueberries
1 cup sugar
½ cup all-purpose flour
½ cup whole wheat flour
1 teaspoon cinnamon
Pinch of nutmeg
1 ½ teaspoons baking powder
½ teaspoon salt
1 cup whole milk
½ cup unsalted butter, melted

Preheat the oven to 375 degrees. Toss the blueberries with the sugar and set them aside.

In a large bowl, stir together the flours, cinnamon, nutmeg, baking powder, salt, and milk. Stir in the melted butter. Spread the blueberries in an ungreased 8- or 9-inch-square baking pan. Spoon the batter over the blueberries. Bake until the dough rises and is golden, 45 to 55 minutes. Serve warm.

Fresh Blueberry Orange Preserves

Makes 6 to 7 half-pints

Slather this on toast or pound cake. Stir it into yogurt. Brush it over chicken or pork just as it comes from the grill.

2 quarts blueberries, rinsed and picked over
3 tablespoons grated orange zest
½ cup fresh orange juice
4 cups sugar

Prepare a stockpot or canner and jars (see page 51).

Put the blueberries, orange zest, orange juice, and sugar in a large pot set over high heat. Bring the mixture to a boil, stirring gently to dissolve the sugar. Continue boiling for 10 minutes, until the juice has thickened. Watch, and stir gently so the bottom of the pan doesn't scorch. The syrup should reach 221 degrees on an instant-read thermometer. To test for readiness, put a teaspoon of the preserves on a cold plate, and put the plate in the freezer for a few minutes; if the preserves then seem firm to the touch, they are ready.

Ladle the preserves into the hot, sterilized jars, leaving ½ inch of headspace. Wipe the jar rims, center the lids on the jars, and screw on the bands until they are just finger tight.

Process the jars for 10 minutes in enough water to cover the jars by an inch. Turn off the heat, remove the canner lid, and allow the jars to stand in the hot water for 5 minutes before removing them. Cool the jars for at least 12 hours before storing them in a cool, dark place.

Cherries

Local cherries are hard to find and worth going after. Our region boasts tart Montmorency and Balaton cherries that make fabulous pies, preserves, and jams. They flourish in northwestern Michigan and along Lake Superior's shores. Sweet Bing cherries grow best along the coast in the Pacific Northwest. But now researchers at the University of Minnesota and University of Michigan are propagating varieties that combine the best of both sweet and tart. The new Hartland is a little bigger than a tart cherry and deeper in color. It has a distinctly sweet flavor that's great for cooking and eating. You'll find cherries in our markets mid to late summer.

COOK'S NOTE

To pit cherries, press lightly on the outside of the cherry to break the skin just a bit, and then pull out the pit.

1 pint = 2 cups pitted cherries

Cherry Clafouti

Serves 6

This classic dessert is most often made with sweet Bing cherries, but the tart snap of fresh pie cherries makes it sing. If you can't find pie cherries, use sweet cherries and cut back on the amount of sugar.

1 pound pie cherries, pitted
1 ¼ cups whole milk or, for a richer cake, half-and-half
½ cup all-purpose flour
4 eggs, at room temperature
½ cup sugar
Pinch of salt
1 teaspoon vanilla
Confectioners' sugar

Preheat the oven to 350 degrees. Butter a shallow 1½-quart baking dish and arrange the cherries on the bottom of the dish.

In a saucepan set over medium heat, warm the milk until small bubbles appear at the edges. Remove the pan from the heat, and whisk in the flour a little at a time. Continue whisking until all the lumps are gone.

In a separate bowl, whisk together the eggs, sugar, and salt until creamy. Whisk in the milk mixture and the vanilla. Pour the batter over the cherries and bake until browned, about 45 to 50 minutes. Transfer the pan to a rack to cool. Dust with confectioners' sugar, and serve warm.

Quick Ideas

Cherry Almond Muffins: Add a handful of pitted cherries and almond extract to a simple muffin recipe.

Cherry Chicken Salad: Toss pitted cherries into your favorite chicken salad.

Cherry Vinegar: Put 2 cups of pitted cherries in a quart of white wine vinegar, cover, and let stand for 2 weeks. Strain off and bottle the vinegar.

Simple Sour Cherry Preserves

Makes 3 half-pints

Sweet, tart, and bright, these plump cherries and their glistening syrup are delightful slathered on a buttery croissant, folded into whipped cream, spooned over ice cream, or eaten straight from the jar.

3 pounds fresh pie cherries, stemmed and pitted
2 ½ cups sugar
2 tablespoons freshly squeezed orange juice

Prepare a stockpot or canner and jars (see page 51).

In a medium pot, combine the cherries with ¼ cup of the sugar and the orange juice. Cook over medium-high heat, stirring frequently, until the sugar has dissolved, about 2 to 3 minutes. Slowly add the rest of the sugar about ½ cup at a time, stirring so it dissolves between additions.

Bring the mixture to a full boil and cook, stirring frequently, until the mixture reaches 220 degrees on a candy thermometer, about 30 to 40 minutes. Skim off any foam that floats on the surface.

To see if the preserves are ready, place a spoonful on a cold plate, set it in the freezer, and wait a minute. If the edge of the preserves wrinkles slightly when pushed, it's ready. If it doesn't pass the wrinkle test, cook the preserves 1 to 2 more minutes and test again.

Remove the pot from the heat, and ladle the preserves into hot, sterilized canning jars, leaving ½ inch of headspace. Wipe the jar rims, center the lids on the jars, and screw on the bands until they are just finger tight.

Process the jars for 10 minutes in enough boiling water to cover the jars by an inch. Turn off the heat, remove the canner lid, and allow the jars to stand in the hot water for 5 minutes before removing them. Cool the jars for at least 12 hours before storing them in a cool, dark place.

Tart Cherry Sauce for Grilled or Roasted Pork or Chicken

Serves 4 to 6

More than a sauce, this spicy, aromatic glaze packs so much flavor that you'll want to make it a staple in your kitchen. Use it to baste chicken, lamb, pork, and game as they finish cooking in the oven or on the grill. The sauce will keep for several weeks in the refrigerator.

3 tablespoons fresh orange juice
1 teaspoon grated orange zest
1 tablespoon honey
¾ cup dry red wine
¼ cup minced shallot
1 small cinnamon stick
1 cup chicken stock (page 264)
1 pound sour cherries, pitted (about 3 cups)

In a heavy saucepan set over high heat, mix together the orange juice, orange zest, honey, wine, shallot, cinnamon stick, chicken stock, and cherries and cook until the mixture is reduced by half. Reduce the heat, and continue cooking until it is reduced to a thin but rich sauce. Remove the cinnamon stick after cooking.

Drying Fruits and Vegetables

An electric dehydrator is the best tool for drying or dehydrating produce. An oven will work, but most ovens cannot be set below 200 degrees. To keep the temperature that low, the oven door must be propped open. Electric dehydrators are energy efficient and include a fan to circulate air during the drying process.

Maintaining the proper temperature is key to successful dehydrating. If the temperature is too low, bacteria may grow on the food and spoil it; if it is too high, the food will overcook and lose flavor and nutrients.

To prepare vegetables for drying, blanch them quickly and dry them thoroughly. Halve or quarter large vegetables so they will blanch easily. Vegetables should be dried at 130 degrees.

To prepare fruit, wash, pit, and slice it; then set it on the trays in single layers. Dry fruit at 135 degrees.

Dried fruits and vegetables are done when they are leathery, with no pockets of moisture. Vegetables should be tough but crisp; fruit should not show any beads of moisture when torn.

Store dried produce in an airtight container or a freezer bag in a cool (about 60 degrees), dark, dry place.

Cranberries

Wisconsin produces most of the world's fresh cranberries, and they're best when just harvested. The fresher the berries, the milder they taste, so those just harvested are worth seeking out at farmers markets. They are the last fruit of our growing season, available from mid-October through freeze.

COOK'S NOTE

When cooking cranberries, add the sugar last. This keeps them from getting tough.
1 pint = 2 cups cranberries

Quick Ideas

Cranberry-Chocolate Chip Cookies: Toss fresh cranberries into your favorite chocolate chip cookie recipe.

Quick Sauce: In a small saucepan set over medium-low heat, stew 1 cup of cranberries, 1 chopped apple, and ¼ cup of fresh cider. Cook until the cranberries pop and the apple is very soft. Sweeten to taste with honey or sugar (you shouldn't need much).

Cranberry Roasted Chicken: Toward the end of the roasting period, toss cranberries into a pan of roasting chicken.

Cranberry Pork Tenderloins

Serves 4 to 6

Pork tenderloins are delicate, tender cuts that cook in no time; in fact, the danger is that they'll quickly overcook. Cranberries bump up the flavor and color when added toward the end of the sauté.

2 pork tenderloins, about 1 ½ pounds each
Salt and freshly ground pepper
2 tablespoons unsalted butter
½ cup chopped onion
1 cup cranberries
¼ cup dry white wine

Preheat the oven to 350 degrees.

Season the pork with salt and pepper. Melt the butter in a large ovenproof skillet set over medium-high heat. Add the tenderloins and sear, rolling them from side to side, until all sides are browned. Remove the pork from the pan and set it aside.

Reduce the heat to medium, and add the onions and cranberries to the pan. Cook until the onions are wilted and the cranberries pop, about 3 minutes. Stir in the white wine, and scrape to loosen the browned bits from the bottom of the pan. Return the tenderloins to the pan, and baste them with the sauce. Put the pan in the oven, and bake until the pork registers 145 degrees on an instant-read thermometer, about 5 to 10 minutes. Allow the pork to stand 5 minutes before slicing the tenderloins into medallions. Serve with the pan juices and cranberries.

Cranberry Snack Cake

Makes a 9-inch cake

Everyone will beg you for this recipe. It's one of those old-fashioned crowd pleasers: tender and moist yet not too sweet. It's terrific with coffee or milk, or even a light beer or sweet wine.

2 cups all-purpose flour
1 teaspoon baking powder
½ teaspoon baking soda
1 teaspoon cinnamon
½ teaspoon freshly grated nutmeg
½ teaspoon salt
½ cup unsalted butter, at room
temperature
1 ¼ cups sugar
1 teaspoon vanilla
3 large eggs
1 cup plain Greek-style yogurt or
sour cream
1 cup fresh cranberries, chopped
Confectioners' sugar (optional)

Preheat the oven to 325 degrees. Lightly butter and flour a 9-inch-square baking pan.

In a medium bowl, whisk together the flour, baking powder, baking soda, cinnamon, nutmeg, and salt. In a separate bowl, cream the butter and sugar until light and fluffy; then beat in the vanilla. Beat in the eggs one at a time. Beginning and ending with the flour mixture, alternate folding portions of the flour mixture and the yogurt into the butter mixture. Fold in the cranberries. Scrape the batter into the prepared pan, spread it evenly, and then tap the pan to release the air bubbles. Bake until a toothpick inserted in the center comes up clean, about 50 to 55 minutes. Cool the cake on a wire rack. Dust it with confectioners' sugar, if desired.

Fresh Cranberry Ginger Salsa

Makes 2 cups

This zesty salsa is so easy it doesn't need a recipe. Make it once, and you can toss it together on the fly whenever you need a dip for chips, a finish to grilled chicken, or a relish for pâté or cheese.

3 cups whole fresh cranberries
½ cup crystallized ginger

In a food processor fitted with a steel blade, process the cranberries and the ginger until they are both finely chopped. You can store the salsa in the refrigerator for up to 2 weeks.

Currants

Jewel-toned currants are delicate, difficult to ship, and best found at the market in late summer and early fall. They're great for more than making jelly. Toss currants into cakes, sorbet, muffins, and sauces.

COOK'S NOTE

Tiny, gem-like, and too tart to eat out of hand, currants add zing to jams, jellies, and sauces.
1 pint = 2 cups currants

Quick Ideas

Quick Currant Sauce: In a small saucepan set over medium-high heat, cook 1 cup of currants with ½ cup of sugar (or more to taste), smashing the currants with the back of a spoon so they release their juices. Bring to a boil and reduce the liquid by half. Strain off the currant skins before using.

Currant Brandy: Fill a quart jar with currants, add enough brandy to cover the fruit, cover with a tight lid, and let the brandy stand for a month. Strain off the brandy, sweeten it to taste, and decant it into bottles.

Currant Hazelnut Cake

Serves 6 to 8

This recipe relies on ground hazelnuts instead of flour, so it's a real treat for those avoiding gluten. This traditional Hungarian cake is perfect with coffee, dessert wine, or currant brandy.

1 cup unsalted butter, at room temperature, plus extra for greasing the pan
1 cup sugar
3 eggs
1 ½ cups ground toasted hazelnuts (page 265)
2 teaspoons vanilla
1 cup currants, stemmed
Confectioners' sugar

Preheat the oven to 350 degrees. Butter a 9- or 10-inch tart pan with a removable bottom, and line the bottom with parchment paper.

In a large bowl, cream the butter with the sugar until the mixture is pale and fluffy. Beat in the eggs one at a time, beating well after each addition. Fold in the ground hazelnuts and the vanilla.

Spread the dough in the tart pan, and scatter the currants over the dough. Bake until golden and just firm, about 30 minutes. Sprinkle confectioners' sugar over the top, and serve while warm.

Currant Jelly

Makes 8 half-pints

Each August, Bonnie Hoyt would tack this recipe, hand-written on an index card, near the tiny wooden baskets of currants in her stall at the tiny Roseville Farmers Market.

4 pounds fresh red currants, stemmed and rinsed
1 cup water
7 cups sugar
½ cup liquid fruit pectin

Prepare a stockpot or canner and jars (see page 51).

Put the currants into a large pot and crush them with a potato masher. Add the water, and bring the liquid to a boil. Reduce the heat, and simmer for about 10 minutes. Strain the fruit into a large bowl through a jelly cloth or a cheesecloth-lined strainer.

Measure out 5 cups of the strained juice and pour it into a large saucepan set over high heat. Bring the juice to a boil, and stir in the sugar, cooking until it dissolves. Stir in the pectin, and boil the mixture for 30 seconds.

Remove the pot from the heat, and skim any foam from the top. Ladle the hot mixture into hot, sterilized jars, leaving ½ inch of headspace. Wipe the jar rims, center the lids on the jars, and screw on the bands until they are just finger tight.

Process the jars for 10 minutes in enough boiling water to cover the jars by 1 inch. Turn off the heat, remove the canner lid, and allow the jars to stand in the hot water for 5 minutes before removing them. Cool the jars for at least 12 hours before storing them in a cool, dark place.

Golden La Crescent grapes, often pressed for wine, are delicious as a snack or in tarts and pies.

Grapes

Local Concord grapes pack a full-on grape flavor, musty and intensely sweet. White grapes are less hardy and more difficult to grow. Their flavor is less floral but clean and tart (they're grown primarily for wine). Local grapes do not ship or store well, so come fall you will find them not on grocers' shelves but in our farmers markets. You'll need to remove the seeds, but it's worth the extra effort.

COOK'S NOTE

Be careful when working with Concord grapes: they stain.

To seed grapes quickly, hold the grape between your thumb and forefinger, and squeeze it gently so the grape slips out of its skin. Discard the skin; then cut the grape in half and dig the seed out with your fingers.

If you're making jelly, you don't need to seed the grapes. The seeds will release as the grapes warm and burst open and will be removed when you press the mixture through a sieve. 1 pint = 2 cups grapes

Quick Ideas

Grape and Apple Crisp: Toss grapes in with apples when making apple crisp. They add a musty sweetness.

Sparkling Grape Juice: Put several cups of grapes into a bowl and smash them to release the juice. Strain the juice through a sieve to remove the seeds and skin. Sweeten the juice to taste with sugar, and then add equal amounts of dry ginger ale. Serve over ice.

Focaccia with Grapes and Rosemary

Serves 6

This twist on the Italian classic uses local Concord grapes. Try substituting cranberries for the grapes when they're in season.

2 cups all-purpose flour
1 tablespoon active dry yeast
¾ cup lukewarm water
1 teaspoon coarse salt
1 teaspoon sugar
¼ cup extra-virgin olive oil
1 ½ cups grapes, seeded
3 sprigs fresh rosemary, stemmed but not chopped
Sprinkle of freshly grated nutmeg

Concord grapes, musty and sweet, make terrific juice and jelly.

In a large bowl, stir together ¼ cup of the flour, the yeast, and ¼ cup of the water. Let the mixture stand until bubbles form, about 20 minutes.

Add ½ teaspoon of the salt, the sugar, and the remaining ½ cup of the water. Stir in the remaining 1 ¾ cups of flour. Turn the dough onto a lightly floured counter and knead until it is smooth, about 5 to 10 minutes, adding just enough flour to keep the dough from sticking. Place the dough in a well-oiled bowl, and turn the dough to coat it in oil. Cover the bowl, and let the dough rise in a warm place until it has doubled in volume, about 1 hour.

Preheat the oven to 450 degrees.

Punch the dough down, and turn it out onto a floured surface. Roll out a large oval about ½ inch thick. Transfer it to a baking sheet. Make shallow, evenly spaced indentations in the surface of the dough. Brush the dough with olive oil. Press the grapes into the indentations, and sprinkle on the rosemary leaves, nutmeg, and remaining salt. Bake until golden and crisp, about 20 to 25 minutes.

Concord Grape Jam

Makes about 6 half-pints

There is a complex elegance to this jam. It's dark and richly sweet, a little musty—the perfect match to Bent River Camembert-style cheese or a buttery scone.

5 pounds Concord grapes, stemmed
5 cups sugar
¼ cup fresh orange juice
1 tablespoon grated orange zest

Prepare a stockpot or canner and jars (see page 51).

Put the grapes in a large, deep pot, and crush them with a potato masher or a heavy spoon. Stir in the sugar, orange juice, and zest. Set the pot over moderate heat and cook, stirring frequently and skimming off the foam as it rises, until the pulp is broken down, about 20 minutes. Force the jam through a food mill or a fine-mesh sieve set over a large bowl. Discard the remaining solids. Return the jam to the pot and simmer over medium-low heat, stirring occasionally as the mixture thickens. When the jam is thick enough to hold its shape on a chilled plate, remove it from the heat.

Ladle the jam into the hot, sterilized jars, leaving ½ inch of headspace. Wipe the jar rims, center the lids on the jars, and screw on the bands until they are just finger tight.

Process the jars for 10 minutes in enough boiling water to cover the jars by 1 inch. Turn off the heat, remove the canner lid, and allow the jars to stand in the hot water for 5 minutes before removing them. Cool the jars for at least 12 hours before storing them in a cool, dark place.

Melons

Muskmelon, watermelon, honeydew—the bouquet of local melons expands each year. Melons come in during the blistering days of summer when you're eager to turn them into lovely cooling drinks, salads, and desserts.

COOK'S NOTE

Melons are interchangeable. Use a mix of local melons in any of these recipes. Melons vary widely in size.

1 pound = 1 small melon = 2 to 3 cups diced melon

Quick Ideas

Melon Bowls: Use hollowed-out melons as serving containers for mixed fruit, chicken salad, or yogurt and granola.

Curried Fruit: Spice 2 cups of cubed melon with ½ teaspoon of curry powder and 1 tablespoon of lime juice, or to taste.

Spicy Melon Salsa

Serves 4

This recipe is one of those happy accidents. The market was short on good tomatoes but long on wonderful melons that needed to be used in something more interesting than a fruit cup. Melon salsa is great with grilled fish, as a dip for chips, and as a garnish to cold cream soups.

½ cup diced honeydew
½ cup diced cantaloupe or muskmelon
½ cup diced watermelon
1 jalapeño or serrano chili, seeded, deveined, and minced
¼ cup chopped cilantro
1 tablespoon honey
2 teaspoons grated lime zest
1 tablespoon fresh lime juice
Salt and freshly ground pepper

In a medium bowl, toss together the melon, chili, cilantro, honey, lime zest, and lime juice. Season the salsa with salt and pepper to taste. Chill before serving.

Melon and Feta Salad in Mint Vinaigrette

Serves 6

Use a mix of gold and red watermelon, fragrant muskmelon, and honeydew. The feta adds a nice balance of salt and heft to the melon's sweet taste and light texture.

1 cup fresh mint leaves
1 tablespoon honey
1 jalapeño, seeded, deveined, and minced
2 tablespoons lime juice
3 tablespoons sunflower oil or olive oil
Salt and freshly ground pepper
3 cups cubed melon (mixed varieties, if possible)
4 cups arugula
4 ounces crumbled feta cheese

In a blender, process half of the mint leaves with the honey, jalapeño, and lime juice. With the blender on low speed, add the oil in a slow, steady stream. Season the dressing with salt and freshly ground pepper.

Chop the remaining mint leaves, and set them aside.

Toss the melon cubes with just enough dressing to lightly coat them. Arrange the arugula on a large platter or individual plates, and serve the melon on the arugula. Garnish the melon with the feta and chopped mint leaves.

Cool Melon Soup

Serves 4 to 6

Icy cold and refreshing, this is a great soup to start off a dinner party or to sip while watching the sunset from the deck. The carrot juice keeps it from tasting too sweet. Add a hit of vodka or gin for a truly fortified soup.

1 small cantaloupe, cut into chunks
1 cup strawberries, hulled
1 cup raspberries
1 cup carrot juice
1 tablespoon raspberry vinegar or lemon juice
1 tablespoon chopped fresh mint
Pinch of sea salt

Put the melon, strawberries, raspberries, carrot juice, vinegar, mint, and salt in a blender. Purée, but do not liquefy, the soup. Serve the soup chilled and garnished with berries.

Pears

Several different heirloom pear varieties grow throughout the more temperate regions in Minnesota and Wisconsin. Our local Luscious, Moonglow, and Harrow Delight pears are tiny, bumpy, and brown-spotted, and they are the most delicious pears. Smaller than commercial varieties from the West Coast, these are intensely sweet and have a delicate floral scent. They're fabulous paired with local cheeses, especially creamy Gorgonzola- and Camembert-style cheeses, and make a lush pan sauce for pork.

The Golden Spice pear, from the University of Minnesota's tree fruit program, is a hardy, aromatic pear. You'll find these lush beauties in our farmers markets as more gardeners and farmers cultivate them. The pears are especially good roasted or turned into sauce. They have a lovely floral fragrance and a mellow flavor that works especially well with ginger and clove.

COOK'S NOTE

Pears ripen off the tree. To speed the process, put unripe pears in a small brown paper bag, close it, and set it on the counter.

1 pound = 2 to 4 pears = 2 to 3 cups, cored and sliced or diced pears

Quick Ideas

Pear Sauce: Substitute pears for apples in your favorite applesauce recipe.

Oven-Roasted Pears: Slice the pears lengthwise and core them. Brush the pears with oil and sprinkle them with sugar. Roast on a lightly greased baking sheet in a 350-degree oven until the pears are tender, about 15 to 20 minutes.

Patten
Pears
$4/tray

Pear, Thyme, and Port Preserves

Makes 5 half-pints

Pear preserves are a lovely side for wintery squash soups and hearty stews. Use the tender, sweet Moonglow or Delicious pears that grow so well in the Northern Heartland. Spotted and gnarled, these pears are not much to look at, but they sure are delicious.

½ cup dried cranberries
½ cup light brown sugar
½ cup fresh orange juice
¼ cup fresh lemon juice
1 tablespoon orange zest
½ teaspoon ground cinnamon
½ teaspoon grated nutmeg
½ teaspoon ground ginger
Generous pinch of salt
2 pounds pears, peeled, cored, and coarsely chopped
¼ cup port
1 tablespoon chopped thyme

Prepare a stockpot or canner and jars (see page 51).

In a large pot, stir together the dried cranberries, brown sugar, orange and lemon juices, orange zest, cinnamon, nutmeg, ginger, and salt, and set the pot over medium-low heat. Bring to a boil, stirring so the sugar dissolves. Add the pears, cover the pot, lower the heat, and simmer for 10 minutes. Remove the cover and simmer until the preserves thicken, 15 to 20 minutes. To test readiness, put a teaspoon of the preserves on a cold plate. Put the plate in the freezer for a minute. If the preserves hold their shape when pushed with your finger, they are ready. If not, continue cooking and test again. Stir in the port and the thyme.

Ladle the preserves into the hot sterilized jars, leaving ½ inch of headspace. Wipe the jar rims, center the lids on the jars, and screw on the bands until they are just finger tight.

Process the jars for 10 minutes in enough boiling water to cover the jars by 1 inch. Turn off the heat, remove the canner lid, and allow the jars to stand in the hot water for 5 minutes before removing them. Cool the jars for at least 12 hours before storing them in a cool, dark place.

Pear Galette

Makes one 10-inch galette

Here, the pear slices melt sweetly into the tender pastry. Serve this with a sliver of pungent blue cheese or topped with Spirited Whipped Cream (page 265).

PASTRY:

1 ½ cups all-purpose flour

¼ teaspoon sea salt

½ cup plus 2 tablespoons cold unsalted butter, cut into small chunks

⅓ cup ice water, or more if needed

FILLING:

6 to 8 pears, peeled, cored, and cut lengthwise into ½-inch wedges

1 tablespoon melted unsalted butter

2 teaspoons sugar

In a food processor fitted with a steel blade or a large mixing bowl, stir together the salt and flour. Cut in the butter until the mixture contains pea-sized pieces. Slowly add ice water to form a stiff dough. Form the dough into a ball, and wrap it in waxed paper or plastic. Refrigerate for about 10 minutes.

Preheat the oven to 450 degrees. Lightly grease a baking sheet.

Using a lightly floured rolling pin, shape the dough into a rough circle about 14 inches across. Transfer the crust to the baking sheet. Arrange the pears in the center of the crust, leaving the outer 3 to 4 inches of dough uncovered. Fold the edges of the crust over the fruit, crimping the edges as needed. The center of the galette will be open. Brush the crust with melted butter and drizzle what's left over the pears. Sprinkle the sugar over the crust. Bake until the crust is browned and the fruit is tender, about 45 minutes, turning the galette after 20 minutes so it bakes evenly.

Let the galette cool on the baking sheet for about 5 minutes before transferring it to a wire rack to cool completely.

Gingered Pear and Winter Squash Soup

Serves 6 to 8

Make this soup the night before so the flavors can mingle. Made without cream, the soup is lush and rich thanks to the dense, hearty squash.

4 cups vegetable stock (page 264)
1 cup white wine
3 cups sliced leeks, white parts only
¼ cup diced celeriac
2 cloves garlic, minced
1 tablespoon grated ginger, or more to taste
Pinch of freshly grated nutmeg
3 cups peeled, seeded, and cubed (2-inch cubes)
    pie pumpkin or butternut squash
2 cups peeled, cored, and diced pears
Salt and freshly ground pepper
¼ cup chopped crystallized ginger

In a large stockpot, bring the vegetable stock, wine, leeks, celeriac, garlic, ginger, and nutmeg to a boil over high heat. Reduce the heat, and simmer for 3 minutes. Add the squash, and cook until it is very tender, about 20 to 25 minutes. Add the pears, and cook another 5 minutes.

Working in small batches, purée the soup in a blender or with an immersion blender until it is very smooth. If the soup has cooled too much, return it to the pot and reheat it. Season with salt and pepper. Serve the soup garnished with the crystallized ginger.

Quince

Golden and aromatic, quince is an old-fashioned fruit that is astringent until it is cooked; then it mellows and tastes of apples and pears with hints of rose. Quince will work in any recipe calling for apples and pears, but it takes longer to cook than either fruit.

COOK'S NOTE

Quince has a floral essence as it ripens. It should be peeled and cooked with a little sugar. The yellow fruit turns a blushing red when cooked.

1 pound = 2 to 4 quince = 2 to 3 cups sliced, diced, or chopped quince

Quick Ideas

Quince Applesauce: Stew peeled, chopped quince with the apples when making applesauce.

Quince Apple Pie: Toss peeled, chopped quince in with the apples when making a pie or a crumble.

Quince is rare, even at market. It's so aromatic that a bowl of the fruit will fill the kitchen with heady perfume as they ripen. They are great stewed into applesauce.

Spiced Poached Quince

Makes 6 cups

Poached quince makes a lovely topping for ice cream or a fine dessert topped with whipped cream. It will keep for a month in the refrigerator.

2 ½ pounds ripe quinces
1 cup sugar
1 cinnamon stick
6 cloves
¼ cup orange juice
1 tablespoon grated orange zest

Using a sharp paring knife, peel the skins from the quinces, reserving the skins. Remove the centers with an apple corer, and reserve the cores. Slice the quinces into ½-inch wedges.

Place the skins and cores in a saucepan, and cover them with water. Bring to a boil, cover, and simmer for about 30 minutes. Strain the mixture and return the liquid to the pot. Add the sugar, cinnamon, cloves, orange juice, and zest. Stir to dissolve the sugar, and then add the quince. Put a plate or parchment paper over the fruit to keep it submerged. Lower the heat, and simmer until the quinces have turned pink and are slightly translucent, about 2 to 2 ½ hours. If the syrup becomes too thick, add more water as needed. Remove the pan from the heat. Remove the cinnamon stick. Transfer the cooled quince and syrup to a storage container, and place it in the refrigerator.

Raspberries

Lucky us that raspberries come into season twice a year: first, just as the strawberry season is fading and again as apples come into play. Golden, pale pink, ruby red, and black raspberries are so delicious and sweet that it seems a shame to do much more than eat them quickly. Yet, they are so easily turned into jam that the small effort will be much appreciated when January comes around.

COOK'S NOTE

Don't wash raspberries until you are ready to use them. They're so delicate that they fall apart easily.

1 pint = 2 cups raspberries

Arugula and Raspberry Salad in Raspberry Vinaigrette

Serves 4 to 6

Toss sweet raspberries and peppery arugula with a vinaigrette that pulls the bright, contrasting flavors together. Add some cooked chicken, and call this lunch.

6 tablespoons raspberry vinegar (page 44)
¼ cup sunflower oil
Salt and freshly ground pepper
1 large bunch arugula (about 5 cups)
1 cup raspberries (a mix of red and gold, if possible)
½ cup sunflower seeds

In a small bowl, whisk together the vinegar, oil, salt, and pepper.

Combine the arugula and the raspberries, and then toss with just enough vinaigrette to lightly coat the salad. Sprinkle on the sunflower seeds.

Quick Ideas

Raspberry Spirits: Fill a quart jar with raspberries and add enough vodka to cover the berries. Tighten the lid, and let the jar stand at room temperature for at least a week. Decant the spirits into clean jars, and discard the berries.

Coulis: Put the berries in a small pot, mash them with a potato masher or a heavy spoon, and heat over low until their juices are fully released. Add sugar or honey to taste. Using a fine-mesh sieve, strain out the seeds. Return the sauce to the pot, and heat until the coulis has thickened. Store the coulis in the refrigerator or freeze it.

Raspberry Vinegar

Makes 4 pints

Raspberry vinegar is the tastiest fruit vinegar and the easiest to make. Use it to deglaze sautéed chicken, or make a refreshing drink by mixing it with club soda or ginger ale.

Black raspberries come into season a little later than red raspberries, and their flavor is deeper and richer. They are a Heartland specialty.

6 pounds raspberries
2 cups white wine vinegar or champagne vinegar
Sugar

Put the fruit into a deep, nonreactive container. Cover the raspberries with the vinegar and stir well. Allow to macerate for 3 days in the refrigerator, stirring occasionally.

Pour the vinegar and raspberries into a jelly bag or a cheesecloth-lined sieve and allow it to drip for at least 6 hours or overnight.

Measure the juice, and put it in a stainless-steel saucepan. Add 1 cup of sugar for each 2 cups of juice. Set the pan over low heat, and stir until the sugar dissolves. Bring the vinegar to a boil, and simmer for about 8 to 10 minutes. Skim. Pour the vinegar into sterilized bottles. Seal and store in a cool, dark place.

Raspberry Jam

Makes 4 half-pints

If you've never made jam before, raspberry is the easiest and quickest of all jams to make. It is also one of the most delicious. You may use black raspberries or blackberries too.

2 pounds fresh raspberries
4 cups sugar (or less if the fruit is very sweet)

Prepare a stockpot or canner and jars (see page 51).

Put the berries into a wide, nonreactive saucepan. Mash them a little, and cook over medium heat until the juice begins to run. Add the sugar slowly, stirring gently until the sugar is fully dissolved. Increase the heat, bring to a boil, and cook for about 5 minutes, stirring frequently.

To test for readiness, put a teaspoon of jam on a cold plate. If it wrinkles when you press it with your index finger, it's set. The jam should reach 220 degrees on an instant-read thermometer.

Ladle the hot jam into the hot, sterilized jars, leaving ½ inch of headspace. Wipe the jar rims, center the lids on the jars, and screw on the bands until they are just finger tight.

Process the jars for 10 minutes in enough boiling water to cover the jars by 1 inch. Turn off the heat, remove the canner lid, and allow the jars to stand in the hot water for 5 minutes before removing them. Cool the jars for at least 12 hours before storing them in a cool, dark place.

Rhubarb

Rhubarb, aka the pie plant, is one of the first plants to appear in the spring. Happily, its season continues as the early strawberries and mulberries appear. They're wonderful partners in pies, cobblers, and tarts. Rhubarb's acerbic nature adds a fine tang to savory sauces and condiments.

COOK'S NOTE

Don't add sugar to rhubarb until after it's cooked. This will help it retain some of its color.
1 pound = 4 cups chopped rhubarb

Quick Ideas

Orange-Ginger Rhubarb Sauce: Put a cup of chopped rhubarb, the juice of one orange, and ¼ cup of chopped crystallized ginger in a saucepan, and simmer until the rhubarb is soft. Sweeten to taste with a little honey, and season with salt and pepper. This is great as a condiment to a cheese plate or spooned over grilled or roasted chicken.

Rhubarb Lemonade: Put about 3 cups of chopped rhubarb into a large glass bowl and cover it with water. Let the rhubarb steep overnight. Strain off the "lemonade" and sweeten it to taste with sugar or honey. Served over ice, rhubarb lemonade is very refreshing. It's also loaded with vitamin C.

Rhubarb Pandowdy

Serves 6

The old-timey word *pandowdy* is about as much fun to say as this homey dessert is to make. It's an upside-down pie, with the fruit's juices bubbling up through the crust to caramelize the top as it cooks. This is an all-rhubarb version, but it's even better with fresh strawberries tossed in.

1 Essential Pastry Crust (page 265)
2 pounds rhubarb, diced into ½-inch pieces
1 teaspoon ground cinnamon
½ teaspoon freshly grated nutmeg
Pinch of salt
½ cup maple syrup

Preheat the oven to 400 degrees.

Roll the dough out so it will fit over a 2-quart baking dish.

Toss together the rhubarb, cinnamon, nutmeg, salt, and maple syrup in the baking dish. Lay the dough over the top of the rhubarb, tucking the edge of the dough between the rhubarb and the inside of the pan to secure it. Bake until the crust is light brown, about 30 minutes. Lower the heat to 350 degrees.

Remove the pan from the oven, and slice crisscrosses in the crust. Return the pan to the oven, and continue to bake another 5 minutes so the juices bubble up to glaze the top as it becomes golden. Serve the pandowdy warm with whipped cream or ice cream.

Roasted Rhubarb Sauce

Makes about 2 ½ cups

For this sauce, you roast the rhubarb so it retains its shape and color while the flavors intensify. This sauce is tart, just a tad sweet, and will work nicely over game, lamb, or pork. It's also terrific served over sorbet, ice cream, or pound cake for dessert.

1 pound rhubarb, cut into 1-inch pieces, about 3 cups
½ pound sugar

Preheat the oven to 400 degrees.

Toss the rhubarb with the sugar and arrange it in a 9 × 13-inch baking dish. Put the dish into the oven, and roast just until the rhubarb is tender (but not falling apart), about 20 to 25 minutes. Let the rhubarb cool, and then scrape it, along with its juices, into a bowl and cover it. Store the sauce in the refrigerator until you are ready to use it.

On signs in the image:
FRESH STRAWBERRIES GREAT FOR:
*Homemade Margaritas!
*Jam, salads, Pie

FRESH BAYFIELD STRAWBERRIES $5⁰⁰ 2 FOR $9⁰⁰

Strawberries

Tiny alpine strawberries are a favorite variety among market farmers and shoppers because their flavor is vibrant and sweet. These are the closest in flavor and looks to those wild strawberries that grow low along paths in the woods. They appear in late June and are in full swing by the Fourth of July.

COOK'S NOTE
Strawberries are porous, so don't hull or rinse them until you are ready to use them.
1 pint = 2 cups sliced strawberries

Quick Ideas

Strawberry Balsamic Sauce: Crush 1 pint of strawberries and sweeten them with a little sugar. Stir in 2 tablespoons of balsamic vinegar. Use this sauce to garnish grilled chicken, lamb, or pork.

Strawberry Clouds: Fold 1 cup of crushed tiny strawberries into 1 cup of whipped cream, spread it in a 9-inch-square cake pan, and pop it in the freezer. To serve, cut into squares and drizzle with chocolate.

Strawberries and Gingered Yogurt: Fold 2 tablespoons of chopped crystallized ginger into 1 cup of plain yogurt and spoon it over strawberries.

Strawberries with Sabayon

Serves 4

A classic Italian sauce, sabayon is a creamy emulsion of egg yolks and dessert wine that turns a simple bowl of strawberries into an elegant dessert.

¾ cup heavy cream
3 tablespoons sugar
2 egg yolks
¼ cup Riesling
1 pint strawberries, rinsed and hulled

Set aside a big bowl of ice. In a medium-size bowl, whip the cream until medium-stiff peaks form. Refrigerate the whipped cream.

In a small stainless-steel bowl, whisk the sugar into the egg yolks until their color lightens. Set the bowl over a saucepan of simmering water, and continue whisking the mixture until it begins to thicken. It is ready when it is light in color and trails off the whisk in ribbons (be careful not to overcook). Remove the bowl from the heat, and whisk in the wine. Set the bowl over the bowl of ice, and whisk until the sabayon is completely cooled, about 5 minutes.

When the sauce is thoroughly cooled, fold in the whipped cream and refrigerate until stiff, about 2 hours. Serve the sabayon over the strawberries in a pretty glass dish or individual goblets.

Strawberry Crisp

Serves 4

What's more comforting than fresh, warm strawberry crisp? This one is light and crisp thanks to the panko topping. Make sure to serve it with plenty of vanilla ice cream melting over the top.

2 pints fresh, local strawberries, hulled, rinsed, and halved
1 ¼ cups panko breadcrumbs
¼ cup powdered sugar
½ teaspoon cinnamon
Pinch of salt
¼ cup chopped blanched almonds
2 tablespoons melted butter
2 tablespoons granulated sugar

Set a rack in the middle of the oven, and preheat the oven to 375 degrees.

Toss the strawberries with ½ cup of the breadcrumbs and the powdered sugar, cinnamon, and salt. Scrape the strawberries into an 8-inch-round baking dish or a square cake pan.

In a separate bowl, combine the remaining breadcrumbs, almonds, butter, and granulated sugar. Sprinkle the breadcrumb mixture evenly over the berries. Bake until the berries are bubbling, about 40 minutes. Let the crisp cool for about 10 minutes before serving it with vanilla ice cream or whipped cream.

Strawberry, Basil, and Balsamic Preserves

Makes 6 half-pints

These sweet and savory preserves will rival any from a fancy gourmet shop. Make them in late June or early July when the tiny local berries are at their peak.

2 pounds strawberries, rinsed and hulled
5 cups sugar
5 tablespoons balsamic vinegar
2 tablespoons chopped basil leaves

Prepare a stockpot or canner and jars (see page 51).

Put the strawberries in a large, deep, heavy pot, and set the pot over medium heat. Once the juices begin to boil, stir in the sugar and cook until dissolved. Reduce the heat, and simmer until the preserves have thickened, about 35 to 40 minutes. To test for readiness, put a spoonful of preserves on a cold plate and set it in the freezer for a minute. If the preserves hold their shape, they are ready. If not, continue cooking. Remove the pot from the heat, and stir in the balsamic vinegar and the basil.

Ladle the preserves into hot, sterilized jars, leaving ½ inch of headspace. Wipe the jar rims, center the lids on the jars, and screw on the bands until they are just finger tight.

Process the jars for 10 minutes in enough boiling water to cover the jars by 1 inch. Turn off the heat, remove the canner lid, and allow the jars to stand in the hot water for 5 minutes before removing them. Cool the jars for at least 12 hours before storing them in a cool, dark place.

Farmers bring the fruits of their fields and their kitchens to market. If you don't have time to make pickles, preserves, and jellies at home, find homemade goodies here at the market.

In the Can

Pickles, preserves, jams, and jellies are easy to put up. Follow these key steps to guarantee your success with canning. You'll appreciate the sunny flavor of your home-grown produce when January winds blow.

Many recipes specify pickling salt – that is, salt without iodine or anticaking agents that will cloud the brine. You can find pickling salt in most supermarkets; if not, use rock salt or kosher salt.

1. Wash the jars, lids, and bands in hot soapy water, and rinse them well. Keep the jars warm until they are ready to use. This helps prevent them from breaking when they are filled with hot liquid. Keep them in a pot of simmering water, a heated dishwasher, or an oven set at its lowest temperature.
2. Fill a stockpot or a canner with enough water to cover the jars by at least 1 inch and heat it to a simmer (180 degrees).
3. Follow the recipes for the recommended amount to fill the jars. Each jar needs space between the food and the jar's rim (called headspace) to allow the food to expand. Most recipes specify ½ inch of headspace.
4. After you fill the jar, remove the air bubbles by sliding a small, nonmetallic spatula inside the jar and gently pressing the food against the opposite side of the jar. Air bubbles inside the jar can affect the canning process, resulting, for example, in unsealed jars or discolored food.
5. Wipe any food from the rims of the jars. Center a new, clean lid on the jar; then twist on the band until it is finger tight. Do not screw the tops on too tightly because the air inside the jar must be able to escape during processing.
6. Place the filled and sealed jars into a canning rack, and then lower them into the pot of boiling water, making sure they are covered by at least 1 inch of water.
7. After processing the jars for the amount of time recommended in the recipe, turn off the heat and let the jars stand in the water for at least 5 minutes. Remove the rack and jars from the water, and allow the jars to cool for 12 hours. Do not retighten or overtighten bands that may have come loose during canning, as that will interfere with the sealing process.
8. Press on the center of the cooled lid. If the jar is sealed, the lid will not flex up or down.
9. Store the sealed jars in a cool, dark pantry for up to a year.

Check with your local university's extension service for more information about canning, or look at Web sites such as www.vegetablegardener.com. There are many books and resources on canning.

Freezer Jam and Jelly
Follow the process described here through step 6; then allow the jars to cool to room temperature. Store the jars in the freezer. When you are ready to use them, allow the jar to come to room temperature (do not microwave).

Canning with a Pressure Cooker
Canning with a pressure cooker is quick and – once you get the hang of it – easy. But every model has different requirements. You will need to learn how to operate the pressure canner by reading the owner's manual. If you have a used pressure cooker, you will have to obtain a manual from the company; provide the model number, and a manual should be sent to you free of charge.

Vegetables

Artichokes

Artichokes? Yes. Local growers are raising cold-hardy artichokes. They're spindly and little but plenty tasty. Our artichoke season, from the end of July through August, is short and unpredictable.

COOK'S NOTE

Most of our artichokes are far smaller than the big California globe artichokes.

To prepare artichokes, trim away the thorns and scoop out the choke. Rub lemon or vinegar on the cut surfaces or fill a bowl with water and add a squeeze of lemon juice or a splash of vinegar and salt to hold the artichokes after trimming. With a sharp paring knife or scissors, trim 1 inch off the top of the artichoke and remove any barbed leaf tips.

Simmer artichokes in a pot with a little lemon, vinegar, and salt and enough water to completely submerge the artichokes. Put a plate over the artichokes to keep them submerged as they cook.

1 pound = 3 to 6 artichokes

Quick Ideas

Roasted Artichokes: Prepare the artichokes, and then remove the outer leaves until you reach the yellow, tender central leaves. With a paring knife, work down to the artichoke's heart. Cut the artichokes in half lengthwise, and scoop out the chokes with a teaspoon. Toss the artichoke halves with sunflower oil or olive oil, and set them on a baking sheet. Roast in a 350-degree oven until very tender, about 15 to 20 minutes.

Stuffed Artichokes: Prepare the artichokes, remove the inner leaves and heart, and reserve the hearts for roasting (see left). Fill the artichokes with chicken salad or roasted, chopped vegetables.

They don't particularly like it here, but artichokes will grow if you give them enough shelter and light. —GAIL SMITH, DragSmith Farms (Barron, Wisconsin)

Pan-Roasted Artichokes with Lemon and Parmesan

Serves 4

Here, the artichokes cook on the stove in just enough butter to keep them moist and add flavor. A shot of lemon juice and a sprinkle of sharp cheese finish them off. Serve this as a side dish, or toss the artichokes with pasta for a light meal.

4 to 8 artichokes, depending on size
3 tablespoons unsalted butter
Juice of half a lemon
2 tablespoons chopped parsley
2 tablespoons grated Parmesan
Salt and freshly ground pepper

Remove the outer leaves until you reach the yellow, tender central leaves. Cut the artichokes in half lengthwise, and scoop out the chokes with a teaspoon. Then cut the artichokes into quarters or eighths; the wedges should be about 1 to 2 inches thick.

Melt the butter in a large skillet set over medium-high heat, and sauté the artichokes, turning them occasionally, until they brown on all sides. Squeeze the lemon juice over the artichokes, cover the pan, lower the heat, and cook the artichokes until they become tender, about 5 to 10 minutes. Peek halfway through; if the pan is becoming dry, add a few tablespoons of water. Remove the artichokes, and toss them with the parsley and cheese. Season with salt and pepper.

Arugula

Arugula's long, scalloped leaves pack a peppery kick that gets stronger through the season. It's related to watercress and radishes—all members of the mustard family. Because arugula likes damp, moderate temps, it grows well in the spring and is seeded again for a fall crop. It's one of the last fresh greens to appear before frost.

COOK'S NOTE

Be gentle with arugula to avoid bruising its delicate leaves. It can trap grit and dirt and needs a good rinsing under cold water before being spun dry in a salad spinner or patted dry with a towel.

1 pound = 10 to 12 cups arugula

Quick Ideas

Grilled Steak: Toss a handful of arugula on steak as it comes hot off the grill. Finish the dish with a drizzle of extra-virgin olive oil and a sprinkling of coarse salt.

Pasta: Immediately after draining it, toss the hot pasta with handfuls of arugula, enough extra-virgin olive oil to coat the pasta, and lemon juice to taste. Season with coarse salt and freshly ground pepper.

Pizza: Spread a handful of arugula on a hot pizza as it comes from the oven. It's especially good on pizzas with sausage, caramelized onions, and chèvre or Manchego cheese.

It's a delicious green and a spicy herb. I use it in salads and as a seasoning.

—LAURA FRERICHS, Loon Organics (Hutchinson, Minnesota)

Arugula Mint Pesto

Serves 4

Arugula makes a snappy pesto that is great stirred into pasta or rice, spread on a pizza, or swirled into mayonnaise for a dip or a sandwich spread. For a zestier spread, substitute watercress for arugula in this recipe.

4 cups arugula
1 cup packed mint leaves
½ cup good-quality olive oil
2 cloves garlic
2 to 3 tablespoons lemon juice
Salt and freshly ground pepper
½ cup shaved hard, aged cheese such as Parmesan, pecorino, or Asiago

Put all of the ingredients into a blender or a food processor and process until smooth. Store the pesto in an airtight container in the refrigerator.

Arugula, Roasted Squash, and Feta Salad

Serves 4

In this salad, the tart, peppery flavors of arugula contrast the gentle sweet notes of roasted squash, the salty feta, and the smooth, zesty lemon vinaigrette.

In place of the squash, try roasted beets, carrots, turnips, or parsnips, alone or combined. In summer, use roasted baby potatoes or carrots instead of the squash.

1 small acorn or delicata squash, peeled, seeded, and cut into 2-inch pieces
1 tablespoon vegetable oil
Coarse salt
8 big handfuls arugula
½ cup chopped fresh mint
½ cup chopped parsley
8 ounces feta or sharp cheese, crumbled or shredded
¼ cup extra-virgin olive oil
Juice and grated zest of 1 lemon
Salt and freshly ground pepper

Preheat the oven to 400 degrees.

Toss the squash with just enough oil to coat it, and sprinkle on a little salt. Spread the squash on a baking sheet. Roast the squash, turning it several times so it doesn't stick to the baking sheet, until it is tender and slightly browned, about 20 minutes.

Toss the arugula with the mint, parsley, and cheese. In a small bowl, whisk together the olive oil, lemon juice, and zest. Toss the salad greens with just enough dressing to lightly coat the leaves. Then toss in the roasted squash, and season to taste with salt and pepper.

Open-Faced Grilled Cheese with Arugula

Serves 4 to 6

Grilled cheese gets a lift from peppery arugula. This makes a fine quick lunch or a side to a bowl of steaming tomato soup.

1 baguette, split lengthwise and lightly toasted
8 ounces thinly sliced mild cheddar, Colby, or Manchego cheese
1 small clove garlic, crushed
2 tablespoons balsamic vinegar
¼ cup olive oil
1 teaspoon Dijon mustard
2 teaspoons honey
6 large handfuls arugula
Salt and freshly ground pepper

Lay the cheese over the baguette and place it under the broiler until the cheese is bubbly and slightly browned, about 2 to 3 minutes.

In a small bowl, whisk together the garlic, vinegar, oil, mustard, and honey. Toss the arugula with just enough dressing to lightly coat it, and season it with salt and pepper.

Top the grilled cheese with the dressed greens just before serving.

The fat asparagus are better tasting, best for the grill.

−Yia Thao, Mill City Market vendor

Asparagus

Suddenly, the asparagus appear. Market tables are laden with bundles stacked high—fat, skinny, purple, white, green. Asparagus are the young shoots of a fast-growing perennial with frilly, fern-like leaves. Ivory asparagus are grown covered in soil; purple stalks turn green when cooked. The difference between fat and slim stalks is a matter of personal preference. The season is short, so don't wait.

COOK'S NOTE

To ready the stalks, gently bend several spears to find the natural breaking point where the tenderness ends and the toughness starts. Then trim the remaining stalks at the same point. If the spears are thick and seem fibrous, use a vegetable peeler or a paring knife to peel them, stopping about an inch below the tips.

1 pound = 2 to 3 cups diced stalks

Quick Ideas

Grilled Asparagus: Lightly coat the asparagus with oil. Place it crosswise to the grate openings on a medium-hot grill, rolling the asparagus to keep it from burning. Remove when the asparagus is slightly charred and tender-crisp. Drizzle with lemon juice and sprinkle with coarse salt.

Shaved Asparagus Salad: Using a very sharp knife or a mandolin, cut the asparagus into thin shards. Toss with a little extra-virgin olive oil, lemon juice, coarse salt, and freshly ground pepper. Top with shaved Parmesan.

Asparagus with Lemon Garlic Mayo: Blanch the asparagus spears in rapidly boiling water just until they are bright green, about 1 minute. Drain and refresh in ice water. Whisk together good-quality mayonnaise, a clove of garlic (minced), and lemon juice to taste and drizzle it over the asparagus. Garnish the asparagus with chopped basil or parsley.

Grilled Asparagus with Shallots and Orange Slices

Serves 4

Eat these on the deck as the sun is going down, with your fingers, sipping wine. Spring never tasted so good.

1 pound asparagus, woody stems snapped off
1 to 2 tablespoons olive oil
Coarse salt and freshly ground pepper
1 large shallot, sliced about ¼ inch thick
4 very thin orange slices, cut into quarters

Heat a gas grill to high or prepare a hot fire. In a large bowl, toss the asparagus with just enough oil to coat and some salt and pepper. Arrange the asparagus in a grill basket or lay it on a sheet of aluminum foil. Put the shallots over the asparagus, and arrange the orange slices on top. Grill, turning the asparagus occasionally, until the oranges just begin to char and the asparagus is just tender, about 5 to 8 minutes. Serve hot or at room temperature.

Fresh Asparagus Soup

Serves 4 to 6

Perfect for Mother's Day brunch or a spring lunch, this vibrant green soup is delicious hot or cold. The soup is a creamy purée enriched with potato and just a touch of cream.

1 tablespoon butter
3 shallots, chopped
Salt and freshly ground pepper
1 ½ pounds asparagus, trimmed and cut into 1-inch pieces, tips reserved
1 small baking potato, peeled and diced
4 cups chicken stock or vegetable stock (page 264)
2 tablespoons cream
1 tablespoon lemon juice, or to taste

Melt the butter in a deep saucepan, and sauté the shallots until soft, about 3 to 4 minutes. Sprinkle with salt and pepper, and add the asparagus stalks, potato, stock, and enough water to just cover. Bring to a boil, reduce the heat, and simmer until the asparagus and potatoes are tender, about 15 minutes.

While the asparagus and potatoes are cooking, bring a small saucepan of water to a boil and blanch the asparagus tips until they are bright green and tender-crisp, about 1 to 2 minutes. Drain, refresh under cold running water, and set aside.

Purée the soup with an immersion blender or in small batches in a blender until smooth; then transfer it to a large bowl. Pour the soup through a fine-mesh sieve into a clean pot. Warm the soup, stir in the cream, and season with the lemon juice, salt, and pepper. Serve the soup garnished with the asparagus tips.

Pan-Roasted Asparagus

Serves 4

Make these when you're in a hurry. The butter will brown a little and add a nutty flavor to the asparagus. Toss pan-roasted asparagus with pasta and call it dinner.

2 tablespoons unsalted butter
1 pound asparagus, trimmed and cut into 1-inch pieces
1 to 2 tablespoons fresh lemon juice
Salt and freshly ground pepper
1 to 2 tablespoons finely grated Parmesan

Melt the butter in a large skillet over medium-high heat, and then add the asparagus. Cover the pan, reduce the heat to medium-low, and cook the asparagus, occasionally shaking the pan, until tender-crisp, about 5 to 7 minutes. Remove the lid, add lemon juice to taste, and season with salt and pepper. Toss with grated Parmesan just before serving.

Pickled Asparagus

Makes 3 pints

Serve these tart pickled spears with composed salads or deviled eggs or a cheese plate. They taste best after the flavors have had a chance to marry, so give them about a month before you enjoy them.

5 pounds asparagus
2 ¼ cups white wine vinegar
¼ cup kosher salt or pickling salt
2 cloves garlic, slivered
½ teaspoon crushed red pepper
½ teaspoon allspice berries
¼ teaspoon cumin seeds
¼ teaspoon coriander seeds

Trim the asparagus so they are about ½ inch shorter than a pint jar. (The tips should not enter the headspace.)

Prepare a stockpot or canner and jars (see page 51).

Bring a pot of water to a rolling boil, and blanch the asparagus until they turn bright green, about 1 minute. Drain, and refresh under cold water.

In a large saucepan, mix together the vinegar, salt, garlic, crushed red pepper, allspice, cumin, coriander, and 2 ¼ cups water. Bring to a boil, stir until the salt dissolves, and remove from the heat.

Pack the asparagus standing upright into the hot, sterilized pint jars. Fill the jars with the vinegar solution, leaving about ½ inch of headspace. Wipe the jar rims, center the lids on the jars, and screw on the bands until they are just finger tight.

Process the jars for 10 minutes in enough boiling water to cover the jars by 1 inch. Turn off the heat, remove the canner lid, and allow the jars to stand in the hot water for 5 minutes before removing them. Cool the jars for at least 12 hours before storing them in a cool, dark place.

Fresh Beans

Fresh beans include French haricots verts (slender and delicate), Italian beans (big, broad, and meaty), gigantic Chinese long beans, and ordinary green and wax beans that may also be purple, red, black, and striped (but turn green when cooked). The name string bean comes from a time when tough fibers ran down the seams, but the strings have long since been bred out.

COOK'S NOTE

To prepare green beans, simply snip off the tough tops and tails.

1 pound = about 3 to 4 cups cut beans

Quick Ideas

Best Green Beans Ever:
Get a big pot of water going, and boil the beans until they are bright green and more tender than crisp (to some, they'll seem slightly overcooked). After draining the beans, drizzle them with good peppery olive oil and sprinkle on some coarse salt.

Sesame Roasted Beans:
Toss the green beans with just enough vegetable oil to lightly coat them. Spread the beans on a baking sheet, and roast them in a 425-degree oven until they are nicely browned and shriveled, about 20 to 25 minutes. Toss the beans with dark sesame oil, coarse salt, and toasted sesame seeds.

Pan-Roasted Dilly Beans:
In a large skillet, melt a tablespoon of butter and sauté a chopped shallot. Add enough water to coat the bottom of the pan, and then add a handful or two of green beans with 2 tablespoons of chopped fresh dill. Toss the beans, cover the pan, and steam the beans until they are just tender, about 5 minutes. Season with salt and freshly ground pepper.

Heartland Salad Niçoise

Serves 4

Local smoked whitefish or trout replaces the canned tuna and olives in this salad. The beauty of this salad is really its eye appeal. It should be composed, not tossed, and look hearty enough for a full meal.

SALAD:

½ pound green beans, tailed and tipped

4 small Yukon Gold or red potatoes

1 head leaf lettuce

Handful of cherry tomatoes, halved (use a mix of yellow and red)

2 hard-boiled eggs, quartered

1 yellow bell pepper, seeded and cut into strips

6 ounces smoked whitefish or trout, boned, skinned, and cut into small chunks

VINAIGRETTE:

2 tablespoons fresh lemon juice

1 teaspoon Dijon mustard

Salt and freshly ground pepper

⅓ cup extra-virgin olive oil

Bring a pot of water to a boil, and cook the beans until they are tender but still crisp. Remove the beans from the water with a slotted spoon and set them aside. Add the potatoes to the boiling water, and cook until they are fork-tender, about 10 to 15 minutes, depending on their size. Drain and cool the potatoes, and then cut them into quarters.

Arrange the lettuce leaves on a large platter or individual salad plates, and compose the beans, potatoes, tomatoes, eggs, bell pepper, and fish on top of the lettuce.

In a small bowl, whisk together the ingredients for the vinaigrette. Drizzle the vinaigrette over the salad.

Chinese Long Beans

Serves 4

Chinese long beans are longer and a bit tougher than our green beans. Their flavor is sharper, their texture a bit crunchier. This recipe uses Asian dried chilies and Szechuan peppercorns, quickly stir-fried to pop their flavors before the beans are added. The dish is fiery!

1 tablespoon sunflower oil or vegetable oil
1 to 2 fresh or dried Asian chilies or 1 to 2 jalapeños, seeded and roughly chopped
1 teaspoon Szechuan peppercorns, lightly crushed
1 pound long beans, trimmed and cut in half, or green beans, trimmed
¼ teaspoon salt
½ teaspoon sugar
3 tablespoons dark sesame oil
Soy sauce

Film a wok or a large skillet with oil, set it over high heat, add the chilies and peppercorns, and stir-fry until fragrant, about 1 minute. Add the beans, and stir-fry vigorously until they turn green and are just tender, about 4 minutes. Leaving the pan on the heat, season the beans with salt and sugar, tossing to coat. Remove the pan from the heat, and toss the beans with the sesame oil and soy sauce to taste.

Shell Beans

Several fresh shell beans, such as edamame, are dual-purpose beans. They can be cooked (whole or seeds only) and eaten as green beans or dried for storage.

Dried shell beans are available in mid-October through the winter. Most need to be soaked before being cooked to add to soups, stews, and gratins.

Fava Beans: Fava beans, aka broad beans, require a little more attention. If you're using them fresh, blanch them and slip off their skins before proceeding with recipes or tossing them into a salad.

Edamame: Fresh soybeans, or edamame, are best when quickly boiled and seasoned with a little soy sauce or salt before serving. To eat them, bite into the end of the bean, pull the pod through your teeth, and draw the soybeans out.

To shell edamame, poke a hole at the end of the pod with your thumb; then zip the pod open. Edamame taste like a cross between sweet peas and lima beans and are lovely tossed into salads, soups, and stir-fries.

Dragon Tongue Beans: These heirloom beans have long, variegated white and pale-pink pods and ivory seeds. When cooked, their colors fade, and they taste like green beans. The seeds, once removed, are nutty and creamy, delicious in soups and stews.

COOK'S NOTE

Unless they're very, very fresh, dried shell beans should be soaked overnight so they cook quickly. Do not add tomatoes or salt to beans until after they are cooked; acid and salt toughen their skins.

1 pound = 2 cups of dry beans or 3 ½ to 4 cups cooked beans

Spicy Edamame

Serves 4

These are the healthiest, best-tasting snack and are terrific with an icy beer.

1 pound edamame, in their pods
2 tablespoons coarse salt
1 teaspoon good curry powder
Generous pinch of crushed red pepper

In a large pot of lightly salted water set over high heat, boil the edamame until they are tender, about 8 to 10 minutes. Drain and set aside.

In a large skillet set over medium-low heat, warm the salt, curry powder, and crushed red pepper, stirring until the spices are hot and aromatic, about 2 minutes. Remove the pan from the heat. Toss the boiled edamame in the warm spices and serve right away.

Fresh soybeans (edamame) are delicious simply steamed or blanched and eaten right out of the pod.

Quick Ideas

Fresh Shell Bean Spread: Remove the beans from their shells, and cook them in boiling water until they are very tender. Purée them in a food processor, adding a little olive oil, fresh lemon juice, and salt and pepper to taste. You'll need about ¼ cup of olive oil per pound of beans. Season the spread with mint and basil, and serve it with crostini or crackers.

Fresh Bean Salad: Remove the beans from their shells, and cook them in boiling water until they are very tender. For each cup of cooked shell beans, add 3 tablespoons of extra-virgin olive oil, 1 tablespoon of lemon juice, ¼ teaspoon of lemon zest, and salt and freshly ground pepper to taste. Toss to combine, and serve on fresh greens.

Spicy Shell Bean Dip: Remove the beans from their shells and cook them in just enough water to cover until they are very soft. Purée 1 cup of cooked beans with 3 tablespoons of olive oil or vegetable oil, 2 tablespoons of chopped jalapeño, and 1 tablespoon of fresh lime juice. Season with salt and freshly ground pepper. Serve the dip with chips or spread it on tortillas.

Fresh Fava Beans and Pasta with Garlic and Prosciutto

Serves 4 to 6

This elegant pasta dish conjures the hills of Tuscany in spring. Fresh fava beans and other broad beans are creamier and more delicate than their dried counterparts. Just be careful not to overcook them.

1 pound small pasta of choice
2 pounds fresh shell beans such as fava beans, cranberry beans, or lima beans
Salt
1 to 2 tablespoons extra-virgin olive oil
3 stalks green garlic, white and light green parts only, sliced, or young onions, sliced
2 ounces prosciutto, cut into strips
¼ cup grated Parmesan or other sharp, aged cheese
2 tablespoons chopped fresh herbs such as basil, thyme,
     and parsley, alone or in combination

Cook the pasta in a large pot of lightly salted boiling water until it's tender but still firm. Drain, reserving about 1 cup of the pasta water.

While the pasta is cooking, remove the beans from their pods. Bring a large pot of salted water to a boil, and cook the beans until they are just tender, about 2 to 3 minutes, depending on the freshness of the beans. Drain the beans, and set them aside.

In a large skillet set over medium, heat the oil and sauté the garlic with a pinch of salt until it is just tender, about 2 to 3 minutes. Add the beans, and warm them for a minute or two.

Stir the pasta into the beans, adding just enough of the reserved pasta water to make a thin sauce. Stir in the prosciutto, cheese, and fresh herbs. Drizzle with a little more oil, and serve right away.

Cranberry Bean Winter Squash Stew

Serves 4 to 6

Uproot Farm (Princeton, Minnesota) sells beautiful Tongue of Fire, a small, creamy cranberry bean. In the summer, they're sold fresh in their striped pods; come fall, they're shelled and dried. Beans, either fresh or dried, shine in this merry mélange of winter vegetables.

1 cup fresh or dried cranberry beans (if dried, soak overnight and drain)
1 small onion, peeled and quartered
1 carrot, scrubbed and broken into 2 pieces
½ cup chopped celery root (celeriac)
1 bay leaf
½ cup farro or barley
2 to 3 pounds squash, seeded, peeled, and diced into ½-inch pieces (about 2 cups)
2 tablespoons sunflower oil or olive oil
Coarse salt
1 large shallot, minced
2 cloves garlic, minced
4 sage leaves, minced
¼ cup minced parsley
1 cup chopped fresh or canned tomatoes
Pinch of crushed red pepper
½ cup white wine
Salt and freshly ground pepper
½ cup grated Parmesan

Put the beans in a large pot with 3 cups of water, and add the onion, carrot, celery root, and bay leaf. Bring to a boil, lower the heat, and simmer until the beans are tender. (Start checking after about 20 minutes.) Remove and discard the onion, carrot, celery root, and bay leaf. Do not drain the beans.

To cook the farro, put it in a pot and cover it with 2 cups of water. Bring the water to a boil; then reduce the heat to a simmer and cook until the grains open and are tender. Farro will cook in 15 to 20 minutes; barley will take about 45 minute to 1 hour.

Preheat the oven to 375 degrees. Toss the cubed squash with 1 tablespoon of the oil and sprinkle it with a little salt. Spread out the squash on a baking sheet so that none of the pieces touch. Roast the squash, turning and shaking the pan so the pieces don't stick, until it is tender and nicely browned, about 20 to 25 minutes.

In a heavy-bottomed pot, heat the remaining tablespoon of oil over medium and sauté the shallots, garlic, sage, and parsley until the shallots are very tender, about 10 minutes. Add the squash, tomatoes, crushed red pepper, and wine and cook for 5 minutes. Stir in the beans, plus ½ cup of their cooking liquid, and the farro. Reduce the heat, and simmer until the liquid is reduced and the stew is thick. Season with salt and pepper. Serve hot with Parmesan sprinkled on top.

These fresh shell beans are as good fresh as they are shelled and dried.
From left to right are cranberry beans, yellow beans, and green beans.

Market Bean Soup

Serves 4 to 6

To make a good, honest bean soup, don't be timid with the garlic and do be generous with the crushed red pepper. The quantities given here are a starting point. This kind of soup always tastes better the next day, so make it ahead if possible.

1 cup fresh or dried shell beans (if dried, soak overnight and drain)
6 cups water
Pinch of crushed red pepper
1 small bay leaf
Salt and freshly ground pepper
1 large onion, diced
2 large fresh tomatoes, diced, or 2 cups canned diced tomatoes
2 cloves garlic, chopped
1 teaspoon chopped rosemary
3 slices salami, cut into strips (optional)
Extra-virgin olive oil

In a large pot set over medium heat, bring the beans, water, crushed red pepper, bay leaf, and a little salt and pepper to a boil. Reduce the heat and simmer for about 10 to 20 minutes, or until the beans are tender. Add the onions, tomatoes, garlic, and rosemary, and simmer until the vegetables are tender, about 20 to 30 minutes.

Purée half of the soup in a blender; then return it to the pot and stir in the salami. Serve the soup drizzled with olive oil.

Bean Sprouts

Those plump, distinctive silver sprouts with yellow "horns," best known as bean sprouts, are the sprouted seeds of the mung bean plant. The Chinese have been growing them for more than three thousand years; we have a bit of catching up to do. Bean sprouts are low in calories and contain a surprising amount of protein and vitamin C.

COOK'S NOTE

You may also find a number of other sprouts at market—adzuki, garbanzo, lentil, pea, and peanut, to name a few. Use them as soon as you get them home: they don't last long.

1 pound = 6 cups bean sprouts

Korean Bean Sprout Salad

Serves 4 to 6

1 pound bean sprouts
1 cucumber, peeled, seeded, and
   cut into matchsticks
1 clove garlic, minced
1 green onion, chopped
Pinch of crushed red pepper
2 tablespoons rice wine vinegar
1 tablespoon sesame oil
1 to 2 teaspoons dark sesame oil
Pinch of sugar
Salt and freshly ground pepper

Put the bean sprouts, cucumber, garlic, green onion, and crushed red pepper in a medium bowl. In a small bowl, whisk together the vinegar and sesame oil. Whisk in dark sesame oil to taste, and then add a pinch of sugar. Toss the dressing with the vegetables, and season the salad with salt and freshly ground pepper.

Quick Idea

Garnishes: Toss on top of soups, stews, and stir-fries at the last minute to add a little crunch.

Beets and Beet Greens

Peaking in late summer and early fall, sweet, earthy beets come in a range of gorgeous hues—magenta, gold, pink, striped (Chioggia). Beets are great served hot or cold, in soups, salads, and roasts. Dark, bitter beet greens enliven soups, stir-fries, and stews.

Beets are best cooked whole, peeled, and then sliced, chopped, or diced. Roasting beets intensifies their flavor and color. Set whole beets on a baking sheet and roast them in a 350-degree oven until they are tender, about an hour. Let the beets cool a bit before peeling them.

Beet greens are loaded with vitamins and antioxidants. Cook them in stir-fries and soups as you would chard (page 106). They're slightly bitter and provide contrast in color and flavor to whole beets.

COOK'S NOTE

Cook beets and their greens separately. Like kale, collards, and chard, beet greens are great in soups and stews and sautéed. Beets are wonderful roasted or steamed. They need about 45 minutes to 1 hour to cook and should be so tender they're easily pierced with a paring knife. Note that different sized beets require different cooking times.

1 pound = 5 to 10 beets = 2 ½ cups diced

1 pound = 8 to 10 cups beet greens

It just makes sense to use beets and beet greens together; the assertive, peppery greens work nicely with sweet, earthy beets.

—Adam Cullip, Loon Organics, Mill City Market

Beets and Beet Greens, North African Style

Serves 4

Inspired by traditional North African flavors, this dish is sweet, savory, and very pretty. It makes a nice addition to a simple dinner of grilled chicken or tofu.

4 to 5 large or 8 to 10 small beets, greens stemmed and sliced into 1-inch strips
½ cup dried fruit (cherries, cranberries, raisins, or chopped apricots)
3 tablespoons extra-virgin olive oil
2 shallots, chopped
2 tablespoons fresh orange juice
1 tablespoon orange zest
½ teaspoon cinnamon
Grated nutmeg
1 tablespoon honey
¼ cup chopped mint
Salt and freshly ground pepper

Preheat the oven to 350 degrees.

Roast the beets until they are tender, about 45 minutes to 1 hour, depending on the size of the beets. When the beet are cool enough to handle, peel and slice them into 2-inch chunks.

Plump the dried fruit by covering with hot water for about 15 minutes. Drain the fruit, reserving the soaking liquid.

Heat the oil in a large skillet set over medium heat, and sauté the shallots for a few minutes. Add the beets, and cook for another minute or so. Add the dried fruit plus ¼ cup of the soaking liquid, orange juice, zest, cinnamon, nutmeg, and honey, and simmer for about 2 minutes. Add the greens, and continue cooking until they are wilted, about 2 to 3 minutes. Stir in the mint and salt and pepper to taste. Serve warm or at room temperature.

Quick Ideas

Beet and Blue: Roast several different colors of whole beets in a 350-degree oven until tender, 45 minutes to 1 hour. Peel and slice the beets when they are cool enough to handle. Drizzle with extra-virgin olive oil and red wine vinegar, and sprinkle on salt, pepper, and a little crumbled blue cheese. Serve warm or at room temperature.

Beets with Orange: Shred several medium beets (about a pound), and sauté them in several tablespoons of butter until the beets are tender-crisp. Sprinkle with fresh orange juice, a bit of orange zest, and salt and pepper.

Beet and Beet Green Salad: Remove the greens from the beets and discard the long, colored stems. Slice the greens thinly, and set them aside. Roast several whole beets in a 350-degree oven until they are tender, 45 minutes to 1 hour. Peel and slice the beets when they are cool enough to handle. Sauté the greens in a little olive oil for a few minutes until they are just wilted. Add the sliced beets, and heat through. Drizzle with balsamic vinegar or red wine vinegar, and season with salt and pepper to taste. Serve warm or at room temperature.

Pickled Beets and Red Onions

Serves 4 to 6 or makes 2 pints

There's nothing better for a cold platter of meat or a cheese tray than these magenta, ginger-spiked beets.

20 baby beets, trimmed
2 medium red onions, peeled and cut into thin slices
2 tablespoons honey
$^1/_3$ cup white wine vinegar
2 teaspoons salt
3 slices fresh ginger
$^2/_3$ cup water

In a large pot of rapidly boiling salted water, cook the beets until they are tender, about 15 minutes. Drain and peel.

In a large saucepan, stir together the onions, honey, vinegar, salt, ginger, and water. Bring to a boil over high heat, and then simmer for about 5 minutes.

Pour the hot marinade over the beets, and allow to cool to room temperature. Cover and refrigerate for several hours before serving. (There's no need to refrigerate the beets if you are going to can them.)

To preserve the beets, prepare a stockpot or canner and 2 pint jars (see page 51).

Put the beets, onions, and marinade into the hot, sterilized jars, leaving $^1/_2$ inch of headspace. Wipe the jar rims, center the lids on the jars, and screw on the bands until they are just finger tight.

Process the jars for 10 minutes in enough boiling water to cover the jars by 1 inch. Turn off the heat, remove the canner lid, and allow the jars to stand in the hot water for 5 minutes before removing them. Cool the jars for at least 12 hours before storing them in a cool, dark place.

Greek-Style Beet and Yogurt Salad

Serves 4

A natural with grilled lamb or moussaka, this salad is dressed with yogurt dressing turned a lovely pale pink by the juices of roasted beets.

3 to 4 beets
3 tablespoons extra-virgin olive oil
2 tablespoons lemon juice
2 teaspoons honey
1 garlic clove, crushed
Salt and freshly ground pepper
½ cup Greek-style yogurt or strained whole-milk yogurt
2 tablespoons chopped fresh dill
Salad greens

Preheat the oven to 350 degrees, and then roast the whole beets until they are tender, about 45 to 60 minutes. When the beets are cool enough to handle, peel and cut them into 1-inch slices.

Whisk together the oil, lemon juice, honey, garlic, and salt and pepper. Toss the roasted beets in the dressing while they're still warm. Set the beets aside to marinate about 1 hour, or refrigerate them overnight.

Whisk together the yogurt and most of the dill along with 1 to 2 tablespoons of the beet marinade. Arrange the beets on a bed of lettuce or salad greens and drizzle with the yogurt. Garnish with the remaining dill.

Simple Beet Soup

Serves 4 to 6

The beets go on, spring to fall. This twist on the classic borscht is not at all heavy, but is satisfying enough for a light supper. Be sure to use super-fresh beets for the best-tasting soup.

3 to 4 medium beets
1 tablespoon unsalted butter
1 medium red onion, chopped
4 cups vegetable stock (page 264)
1 sprig thyme
¼ cup heavy cream
Salt and freshly ground pepper
Raspberry vinegar or lemon juice

Put the beets in a large saucepan, and cover them with water. Bring the water to a boil over high heat; then reduce the heat and simmer until the beets are tender, about 50 to 60 minutes. Drain the beets, and allow them to cool. Peel the beets, and cut them into a rough dice.

Melt the butter in a medium saucepan over medium heat. Add the onions, and cook until the onion is tender and translucent, about 15 minutes. Transfer the onions and half of the beets to a blender, add enough stock to cover, and process to make a smooth purée.

Return the purée to the saucepan along with the remaining stock and thyme. Turn the burner to medium-low and simmer the soup for 10 minutes. Remove the thyme, add the remaining beets and the cream, and season to taste with salt, pepper, and a splash of raspberry vinegar.

Bitter Melon

Don't let its looks deceive you. Though bitter melon resembles a pale wart-covered cucumber, its assertive bitter flavor is essential to authentic Indian, Asian, and Filipino cuisine. Its acerbic taste and crunch balance rich, spicy foods. The health benefits of bitter melon are legendary; in fact, the National Bitter Melon Council (http://bittermelon.org/) is devoted to providing such information.

COOK'S NOTE

Unlike cucumber or zucchini, bitter melon is better when it is a little past its green prime: the more mature melons are less bitter. At the market, look for large, pale bitter melons. To tame the bitterness, remove the seeds, salt the slices, and let them drain in a colander for about 15 to 20 minutes. Rinse, and then pat the slices dry with a towel.

1 pound = 1 ½ cups seeded and sliced bitter melon

Quick Ideas

Simple Stir-Fry: Prepare the bitter melon as directed in the Cook's Note. Toss it into your favorite stir-fry dish to add a note of bitterness.

Thai-Style Scrambled Eggs: Prepare the bitter melon as directed in the Cook's Note. Heat some oil in a skillet, stir-fry the bitter melon until it is lightly browned, add several beaten eggs, and cook until they're just set. Season with soy sauce, and serve right away.

Bitter Melon Stir-Fry

Serves 4

Mai Vang, a college freshman who helps her mom and her grandmother at their family's St. Paul Farmers Market stand each year, translated her grandmother's instructions for making this dish. It's a snap to make and good alongside grilled chicken or fish.

1 pound bitter melon, seeded and sliced
Coarse salt
1 to 2 tablespoons sunflower oil or vegetable oil
2 cloves garlic, minced
Generous pinch of crushed red pepper
2 tablespoons soy sauce
1 tablespoon rice wine vinegar
1 teaspoon brown sugar

Toss the bitter melon slices with a little salt, and place them in a colander. Let the bitter melon drain for about 15 to 20 minutes. Rinse with cold water, and pat dry.

Film a large skillet or wok with the oil, set it over medium-high heat, and stir-fry the garlic and crushed red pepper quickly before tossing in the bitter melon. Stir-fry until the bitter melon begins to brown slightly, and then add the soy sauce, vinegar, and sugar.

Bitter Melon Salad

Serves 4 to 6

This dish is as much a salad as a condiment. The vegetables marinate in a hot, sweet dressing that just tastes better with time. Pile it on top of grilled steak or pork. Serve it alongside grilled fish. It keeps several days in the refrigerator.

1 pound bitter melon, seeded and thinly sliced
Coarse salt
1 onion, thinly sliced
1 red or green bell pepper, seeded and thinly sliced
1 inch ginger, peeled and thinly sliced
2 tablespoons rice wine vinegar
2 tablespoons hoisin sauce
2 tablespoons sunflower oil or vegetable oil
1 teaspoon dark sesame oil, or more to taste
1 teaspoon brown sugar
Salt and freshly ground pepper

Toss the bitter melon slices with a little salt, and set them in a colander to drain for about 15 to 20 minutes. Rinse, and pat dry with a towel. Turn the bitter melon into a medium bowl, and toss in the onion, bell pepper, and ginger.

In a small bowl, whisk together the vinegar, hoisin sauce, oils, and sugar. Toss the vegetables with the dressing, and season with salt and pepper. Let the salad stand about 30 minutes before serving.

Bok Choy

With its broad leaves and satiny white stalks, bok choy is the most tender member of the cabbage family. The only trick is to not overcook it, letting the delicate flavors and crunchy texture shine.

COOK'S NOTE

1 pound = 4 to 6 cups sliced bok choy

Quick Ideas

Sesame Stir-Fry: Cut the stalks into 1-inch pieces, and stir-fry or sauté them in a little oil over high heat until tender but still crisp, about 3 to 6 minutes. Drizzle on a little dark sesame oil, sprinkle with toasted sesame seeds or toasted almonds, and season with salt and pepper or soy sauce.

Dips for Bok Choy: Use bok choy stems instead of celery for dipping into Maple Mustard Vinaigrette (page 263) or Asian Peanut Sauce (page 163).

Bok Choy Slaw: Slice the bok choy leaves very thin. Toss them with shredded mint, basil, extra-virgin olive oil, and fresh lemon juice.

Bok Choy and Crispy Tofu

Serves 4

This tofu fries up crisp on the outside and creamy within, a perfect foil to the delicate, crunchy bok choy. Serve over Chinese curly noodles or rice.

16 ounces firm tofu, cut into 1-inch slices
1 (10-ounce) package Chinese curly noodles or 1 ½ cups rice
3 tablespoons vegetable oil
1 teaspoon crushed red pepper
1 ½ to 2 pounds baby bok choy, coarsely chopped
6 cloves garlic, minced
1 yellow bell pepper, seeded and thinly sliced
¼ cup white wine or vegetable stock
2 to 3 tablespoons soy sauce
2 teaspoons honey, or to taste
1 small jalapeño, seeded and thinly sliced

Place the sliced tofu on linen or paper towels, cover it with more towels, and then place a cookie sheet weighted with heavy pans on top to press out excess liquid. After 10 to 15 minutes, remove the pans and towels and cut the tofu into 1-inch cubes.

Meanwhile, prepare the noodles or rice. Chinese curly noodles should boil for about 4 or 5 minutes; simmer white rice for about 20 minutes, brown rice for about 30 minutes.

Heat the oil and the crushed red pepper in a large skillet or a wok set over medium-high heat. Sauté the tofu, turning the cubes often, until it is golden brown. Put the tofu on paper towels to drain, and set it aside.

Toss the bok choy into the skillet, stir quickly, then add the garlic, bell pepper, wine, soy sauce, honey, and jalapeño, and cook until the bok choy is just tender, about 1 to 2 minutes. Toss in the tofu. Serve over cooked rice or noodles.

Bok Choy, Radish, and Orange Salad with Cilantro

Serves 4 to 6

Crunchy, nutty, and just a little sweet, this salad is made for a sweltering summer night. Allow a little time for the flavors to marry before serving it icy cold.

2 oranges
1 clove garlic
2 tablespoons raspberry vinegar or white wine vinegar
Large pinch of cayenne
2 to 3 tablespoons extra-virgin olive oil
1 large or 2 small heads bok choy, thinly sliced
8 small red radishes, cut into thin rounds
5 scallions, white and light green parts thinly sliced
1/3 cup fresh cilantro leaves
2 tablespoons mint leaves, thinly sliced

Grate 1 teaspoon of zest from an orange, and set it aside. Peel the oranges, being sure to remove all the bitter white pith, and slice them into wheels.

To make the dressing, mash the garlic in a small bowl, or use a mortar and pestle, and then work in the vinegar and cayenne. Whisk in the olive oil and the orange zest.

Place the bok choy on a large serving platter or individual serving plates. Arrange the orange slices and radishes on top of the bok choy. Drizzle with the dressing, and scatter the scallions, cilantro, and mint over top.

Broccoli

The Italians know how to cook broccoli; in fact, they introduced it to the St. Paul Farmers Market about sixty years ago. The most familiar variety is sprouting broccoli, with its thick central stalk and head of florets. Broccolini, with its smaller florets and longer thin stalks, is a little bit sweeter and tastes like a cross of broccoli and asparagus. Rapini, or broccoli rabe, although it has the same frilly foliage, is not broccoli at all but a cousin of the turnip. It's stronger and more assertive than broccoli or broccolini.

COOK'S NOTE

Cook the broccoli stems as you do the florets. If they're tough, just peel off the outer layer; then slice thinly and cook as you would florets.

1 pound = 2 cups broccoli florets and chopped stems

Quick Ideas

Roasted Broccoli: Toss broccoli florets and chopped stems with olive oil and sprinkle them with coarse salt. Spread out the broccoli on a baking sheet (keep the florets from touching) and roast at 450 degrees, shaking the pan occasionally, until the edges are browned and crisp. Drizzle with balsamic vinegar or lemon juice before serving.

Butter-Steamed Broccoli: Melt a couple of tablespoons of unsalted butter in a skillet over medium heat, and toss in the broccoli. Cover, and cook until tender-crisp, about 3 to 4 minutes. Drizzle with lemon or lime juice, and season with salt and pepper before serving.

Broccoli and Chickpea Salad: Steam or blanch broccoli florets a few minutes; then refresh them in ice water and drain thoroughly. Toss with cooked or canned chickpeas, good olive oil, and red wine vinegar or lemon juice to taste. Season with crushed red pepper, coarse salt, and freshly ground pepper. Serve chilled or at room temperature.

Roast Broccoli with Red Peppers

Serves 4

The Hmong and Vietnamese growers have shown us how to spice up European vegetables, such as broccoli and cauliflower, to create recipes like this robust side dish. When served over rice or buckwheat noodles, this makes a great vegetarian entrée.

5 cups broccoli florets (about 2 heads broccoli)
2 large red or yellow bell peppers, seeded, deveined, and cut into 2-inch strips
6 fresh red Thai chilies, stems removed
4 tablespoons sesame oil
3 tablespoons toasted sesame oil
Coarse salt
1 to 2 tablespoons fresh lime juice
1 teaspoon grated ginger, or to taste
1 clove garlic, minced
1 tablespoon honey
Salt and freshly ground pepper
2 tablespoons cilantro leaves

Preheat the oven to 450 degrees.

Put the broccoli, bell pepper, and chilies into a large bowl and toss with 3 tablespoons of the sesame oil, 1 tablespoon of the toasted sesame oil, and a little salt. Spread the vegetables on a large baking sheet. Roast, stirring occasionally, until the broccoli and peppers begin to darken, about 20 to 23 minutes.

In a small bowl, whisk together the remaining sesame oil and toasted sesame oil with the lime juice, ginger, garlic, and honey. Adjust the seasonings, adding a little salt and pepper to taste.

Toss the vegetables with the vinaigrette, and sprinkle with the cilantro. Serve warm or cold. You may remove the Thai chilies or leave them in for color, but warn diners not to eat them: they're searing hot!

Broccolini with Chickpeas and Tomatoes

Serves 4

Broccolini, a cross of broccoli and Chinese kale, began showing up in the stalls of market vendors who supply restaurants before we saw it in grocery stores. Chefs favor its delicate stems and distinct peppery bite. Broccolini shines in this recipe, but broccoli and cauliflower work equally well.

1 large head broccolini, cut into florets
2 tablespoons extra-virgin olive oil
1 small onion, diced
4 garlic cloves, chopped
2 large tomatoes, diced (about 2 cups)

1 cup cooked or canned chickpeas, drained
1 tablespoon fresh oregano
2 tablespoons chopped fresh basil
Salt and freshly ground pepper
¼ cup shredded Parmesan or pecorino

In a large pot of rapidly boiling water, blanch the broccolini until it is bright green, about 1 minute. Drain, and refresh under cold water.

Heat the olive oil in a large skillet, and sauté the onion and garlic until they are soft. Add the tomatoes, chickpeas, oregano, basil, and broccolini; cover, and cook until heated through, about 3 to 5 minutes. Season with salt and freshly ground pepper, and serve sprinkled with Parmesan.

Broccoli Gribiche

Serves 4 to 6

Gribiche is just a fancy name for a mayonnaise-like dressing that's made with cooked eggs. This makes a terrific luncheon salad or a nice side salad.

1 pound new potatoes (Yukon Gold, red, or both)
1 pound broccoli, broken into florets
¾ cup sunflower oil
Sea salt
¼ cup apple cider vinegar, or more to taste
1 teaspoon Dijon mustard
1 shallot, chopped
4 hard-boiled eggs, peeled and yolks and white separated
2 tablespoons chopped parsley
2 tablespoons chopped chives

Preheat the oven to 400 degrees.

Cut the potatoes into 2-inch pieces (about the size of the broccoli florets). Put the potatoes and broccoli in a large bowl, toss with enough of the oil just to coat, and sprinkle with a little salt.

Spread out the broccoli and potatoes on one or two baking sheets so they don't touch. Roast until the potatoes are tender and the broccoli is lightly browned, about 20 to 25 minutes.

In a small bowl, whisk together the vinegar, mustard, and shallots. Whisk in the remaining oil. Smash the egg yolks into the vinaigrette to make a smooth paste.

Chop the egg whites and put them in a bowl with the roasted broccoli and potatoes. Toss with just enough of the dressing to lightly coat. Sprinkle the parsley and chives on top. Serve warm or at room temperature.

Brussels Sprouts

Brussels sprouts on their stalks resemble something Dr. Seuss might have dreamed up. The tiniest member of the cabbage family, Brussels sprouts are more versatile and a bit sweeter than their big-headed cousins. Find stalks of Brussels sprouts at our farmers markets.

COOK'S NOTE

Overcooking turns Brussels sprouts into the stuff of bad jokes. If you're steaming or boiling them, be sure to pull them from the stove as soon as they're tender. They're better roasted to a nutty, caramel brown.

1 pound = 2 to 4 cups Brussels sprouts

Caramelized Brussels Sprouts

Serves 4

Roasted to a toasty, caramelized brown, these Brussels sprouts may not make it from pan to table—they're just that good.

1 pound Brussels sprouts, rinsed and trimmed
1 to 2 tablespoons sunflower oil or olive oil
Coarse salt
1 lemon, quartered

Preheat the oven to 400 degrees.

In a medium bowl, toss the Brussels sprouts with just enough oil to lightly coat them and sprinkle on some salt. Roast, shaking the pan occasionally, until the Brussels sprouts are nutty brown, about 15 to 25 minutes. Serve with lemon wedges on the side.

Quick Ideas

Braised Brussels Sprouts: Heat a tablespoon of butter or oil in a heavy skillet, and toss in about a pound of Brussels sprouts (cut them in half if they are large). Toss to coat; then cover and cook, shaking the pan often, until they are slightly wilted but still crunchy. Splash them with a little balsamic vinegar or red wine vinegar, and season with salt and pepper.

Brussels Sprout Slaw: Shred a pound of Brussels sprouts, and toss them with olive oil to coat. Add lemon juice to taste, and season with salt and pepper. Let the slaw stand for about a half hour at room temperature or overnight, covered, in the refrigerator. Right before serving, toss in shredded Parmesan or Asiago cheese and chopped toasted walnuts or pecans.

Pan-Seared Brussels Sprouts: Cut a pound of Brussels sprouts in half. Heat enough butter in a medium skillet to coat the bottom of the pan. Set the Brussels sprouts in the pan cut-side down, and sear them without flipping until they are golden brown and tender, about 10 minutes.

Pickled Brussels Sprouts

Makes 6 pints

No one can top Martha's Joy pickles—cauliflower, broccoli, asparagus, cucumber, and Brussels sprouts. Martha, a vibrant African American woman in her 70s, puts up her garden produce as her mother did down South. Find Martha, smartly dressed, often wearing a hat, at many of the Minneapolis and St. Paul markets, and treat yourself to a jar or two of her delicious wares. If you're lucky, she'll share at least one good pickling secret.

2 ½ pounds Brussels sprouts, trimmed
2 medium yellow onions, thinly sliced
1 quart white wine vinegar or champagne vinegar
2 cups sugar
1 tablespoon salt
1 teaspoon crushed red pepper, or to taste

Prepare a stockpot or canner and jars (see page 51).

Bring a large pot of salted water to a boil over high heat. Blanch the Brussels sprouts until they're bright green, about 3 minutes, and then drain them. Pack the cooked Brussels sprouts and the onion slices into the hot jars.

In a medium nonreactive pot, stir together the vinegar, sugar, salt, and crushed red pepper. Bring the mixture to a boil over medium heat, stirring to dissolve the sugar, and then lower the heat to simmer the liquid gently for 5 minutes.

Remove the brine from the heat, and pour it over the Brussels sprouts and onions, making sure that the crushed red pepper is distributed evenly and leaving ½ inch of headspace. Wipe the jar rims, center the lids on the jars, and screw on the bands until they are just finger tight.

Process the jars for 10 minutes in enough boiling water to cover the jars by 1 inch. Turn off the heat, remove the canner lid, and allow the jars to stand in the hot water for 5 minutes before removing them. Cool the jars for at least 12 hours before storing them in a cool, dark place.

Red and green cabbages make bright slaws, salads, and stir-fries.

Cabbage

You'll find local cabbages, especially red and green heads, at the markets long after snow covers the fields. These store beautifully well into the new year.

Red and green cabbage heads are tight, shred well, and take a little longer to cook than these other varieties:

- Savoy cabbage's leaves are looser and frilly, and the flavor is more delicate.
- Chinese cabbage is crunchy and juicy.
- Mustard cabbage (pak choy) packs a spicy kick.
- Napa cabbage sports long, crisp stems.

COOK'S NOTE

Cabbages are interchangeable. Use any cabbage in these recipes—just adjust the cooking time. Delicate cabbage (such as savoy and napa) cooks quickly.

1 pound = 4 to 5 cups chopped or shredded cabbage

Harvest Cabbage Soup

Serves 4 to 6

"Vinegar is the key," says Ricki Johnson, who helps her mom each Saturday at the St. Paul Farmers Market. "Without good vinegar, cabbage soup just tastes flat." This good advice applies to every recipe for cabbage, cooked or raw.

1 tablespoon sunflower oil or vegetable oil
2 cups shredded red or green cabbage
1 small leek, split lengthwise, rinsed under cold water, and chopped (white part only)
1 cup diced carrot (about 5 carrots)
1 cup diced celery (about 2 large stalks)
1 clove garlic, crushed
1 tablespoon chopped thyme
1 bay leaf
6 cups chicken or vegetable stock (page 264)
Apple cider vinegar
Salt and freshly ground pepper
Yogurt or sour cream

In a large, deep pot set over medium-high heat, heat the oil, and sauté the cabbage, leeks, carrots, celery, and garlic. Cover the pot and cook about 5 minutes. Add the thyme, bay leaf, and just enough stock to cover. Bring the stock to a boil, reduce the heat, and simmer, partially covered, until the vegetables are tender. Add a splash of vinegar and salt and pepper to taste. Serve with a dollop of yogurt or sour cream.

Quick Ideas

Sweet 'n' Sour Cabbage: Melt several tablespoons of unsalted butter in a large skillet, and add several cups of thinly sliced cabbage. Toss, cover, and cook just until the cabbage is tender, about 3 to 5 minutes. Stir in 1 to 2 tablespoons of vinegar, 1 to 2 teaspoons of honey, ½ cup of chopped apple, and ¼ cup of raisins. Season to taste with salt and pepper.

Pan-Seared Red or Green Cabbage: Cut a small head of red or green cabbage into wedges about 1 inch thick, leaving the core intact so the leaves don't fall apart. Heat a little oil in a heavy skillet. When it's hot, sear the cabbage wedges until they are golden brown, about 3 to 5 minutes per side. They should be crispy outside and tender within. Season with salt and freshly ground pepper.

Super Skinny Slaw: Shred a head of red or green cabbage and toss with ½ cup of shredded red onions and 2 shredded carrots. Add about ½ cup of raspberry vinegar, rice vinegar, or cider vinegar, and salt, pepper, and a touch of sugar. Cover and refrigerate overnight before serving.

Asian Slaw

Serves 4

This salad, from Mai Yang, a vendor at the St. Paul Farmers Market, will become a kitchen staple summer through fall. It travels to picnics, can be made ahead, and is easily doubled or tripled for a crowd. Use any combination of cabbage or shredded vegetables.

1 large head napa cabbage, thinly sliced
1 red bell pepper, seeded, deveined, and thinly sliced
1 bunch green onions, thinly sliced
1 cup chopped cilantro
2 tablespoons sliced mint
¼ cup vegetable oil
2 tablespoons toasted sesame oil
2 tablespoons rice vinegar
1 tablespoon grated ginger
1 teaspoon soy sauce, or to taste
2 tablespoons toasted sesame seeds

Toss the cabbage, bell pepper, onions, cilantro, and mint together in a large bowl. In a small bowl, whisk together the vegetable oil, sesame oil, vinegar, ginger, and soy sauce. Toss the vegetables with the dressing, cover, and refrigerate overnight. Serve sprinkled with toasted sesame seeds.

Napa, or Chinese, cabbage's long, frilled leaves are wonderful for rolling around rice and meat stuffing. They braise beautifully too.

Classic Coleslaw

Serves 6

Coleslaw is best made ahead. This recipe is easily doubled to feed a crowd for summer cele-brations—Memorial Day, Fourth of July, Labor Day. For a more colorful salad, use a mixture of green and red cabbage. Yogurt takes the place of sour cream for a lighter, tangier slaw. Be warned though, the mayonnaise is not hot-weather friendly: keep this cold until right before serving.

2 tablespoons Dijon mustard, or more to taste
1 tablespoon sugar
½ cup white wine vinegar
1 cup mayonnaise
½ cup whole-milk yogurt
1 large head green cabbage, shredded
2 carrots, shredded
Salt and freshly ground pepper

In a large bowl, whisk together the mustard, sugar, vinegar, mayonnaise, and yogurt until smooth. Stir in the cabbage and carrots, and season with salt and pepper to taste. Serve cold.

Spicy Pickled Red Cabbage

Makes about 3 quarts

You'll want to start this a day ahead, as the cabbage must stand after being salted. This colorful condiment is great on brats and a must on Reuben sandwiches.

6 pounds red cabbage (about 2 small to medium heads)
¼ cup fine sea salt
2 tablespoons cloves
2 tablespoons allspice berries
2 tablespoons peppercorns
2 cinnamon sticks, broken into pieces
4 cups apple cider vinegar
¼ cup brown sugar
¼ cup mustard seed

Core and then shred the cabbage by hand, on a mandolin, or in a food processor fitted with a slicing blade. In a large, clean crock or a glass bowl, alternate layers of the cabbage with sprinklings of the salt. Cover, and let stand in a cool place for 24 hours.

Turn the cabbage into a colander set over the sink. Rinse it with cool, running water and let it drain. Let the cabbage dry for about 6 hours on trays lined with towels (or paper towels).

Prepare a stockpot or canner and jars (see page 51).

In a large stainless steel pot, stir together the cloves, allspice, peppercorns, cinnamon, vinegar, brown sugar, and mustard seed. Bring the vinegar to a boil, and stir to dissolve the sugar. Reduce the heat, and simmer until the spices have infused the liquid, about 5 minutes. Strain out the spices, and return the liquid to the pot.

Pack the cabbage into hot, sterilized jars, stopping a generous ½ inch short of the jar rim. Ladle in enough hot pickling liquid to cover the cabbage, leaving ½ inch of headspace. Wipe the jar rims, center the lids on the jars, and screw on the bands until they are just finger tight.

Process the jars for 10 minutes in enough boiling water to cover the jars by 1 inch. Turn off the heat, remove the canner lid, and allow the jars to stand in the hot water for 5 minutes before removing them. Cool the jars for at least 12 hours before storing them in a cool, dark place.

Carrots

Rainbows of carrots are the pride of market growers who display ever more shapes, sizes, and colors each year. The Nantes, deep orange and magenta; the Chantenay with its short, thick cone-shaped root; the tiny finger-shaped Bambina; the pointed Horn; the white Bolero—all are crisp, sweet, and complex. Come winter, find heirloom varieties grown to store well; their starches convert to sugar, so they taste even sweeter after a little time out of the field.

COOK'S NOTE

Stored properly (in plastic bags in the refrigerator), carrots keep beautifully, retaining their color and nutrients for a week or so out of the fields.

1 pound = 4 cups shredded or 6 cups chopped carrots

Quick Ideas

Simple, Sweet Carrot Purée: Simmer a pound of chopped carrots in enough salted water to cover until they are very soft, about 15 minutes. Drain and transfer to a food processor or a blender. Purée the carrots with a little heavy cream or sour cream, adding salt, pepper, and nutmeg to taste.

Roasted Carrots: Preheat the oven to 400 degrees. Cut some carrots into thin, long matchsticks. Toss them with just enough olive oil to coat, and sprinkle on a little coarse salt. Spread the carrots on a baking sheet so the pieces do not touch. Roast, shaking the pan occasionally and turning the carrots so they don't stick, until the carrots are nicely browned, about 15 to 20 minutes.

Quick Carrot Slaw: Shred some carrots, and toss them with just a little walnut oil or olive oil, lemon juice, salt, pepper, and a pinch of sugar. Toss in chopped nuts and dried cranberries.

Gingered Carrot Soup

Serves 4 to 6

Make this soup in February when the storage carrots are released; though they were harvested in the fall, these carrots are sweeter than they would have been in October because their starches converted to sugar over the months in storage.

1 tablespoon sunflower oil
1 onion, chopped
1 tablespoon grated ginger
4 cups chopped carrots
1 small potato, peeled and chopped
½ cup apple cider
Pinch of freshly grated nutmeg
Pinch of crushed red pepper
Salt and freshly ground pepper
Chopped crystallized ginger

In a soup pot set over medium-high heat, heat the oil and sauté the onion until it's soft and translucent. Stir in the ginger, carrots, potato, apple cider, and enough water to just cover. Increase the heat, and bring the liquid to a boil. Reduce the heat, and simmer until the vegetables are soft.

Purée the soup in batches in a blender or use an immersion blender. Season the soup to taste with nutmeg, crushed red pepper, salt, and pepper. Serve the soup garnished with chopped crystallized ginger.

Caramelized Carrots with Orange Glaze

Serves 4 to 6

Carrots, pan roasted to a lovely caramel brown, are finished with a simple zesty orange glaze. Serve these carrots with roasted chicken or turkey.

1 pound mixed carrots
1 tablespoon walnut oil, hazelnut oil, or sunflower oil
1 large shallot, minced
¼ cup fresh orange juice
2 teaspoons coarse mustard
2 teaspoons honey
1 tablespoon orange zest
1 tablespoon chopped parsley
Salt and freshly ground pepper

Slice the carrots slantwise into thin ovals. Heat the oil in a large skillet set over medium-high heat, and sauté the carrots in batches, being careful not to crowd the pan, stirring until they are nicely browned. Each batch will take about 5 to 8 minutes. Transfer the sautéed carrots to a medium bowl, and cover it to keep the carrots warm.

Add the shallots to the pan, and sauté until they are soft, 2 to 3 minutes. Whisk in the orange juice, mustard, and honey. Return the carrots to the pan, add the orange zest and parsley, and turn to coat. Season with salt and pepper to taste.

Carrot Salad with Coriander, Cumin, and Cilantro

Serves 4

This light, crunchy salad brightens up the dullest January day. It is especially good when made with winter carrots.

1 clove garlic
1 teaspoon ground cumin
1 teaspoon ground coriander
Pinch of crushed red pepper
¼ cup fresh lemon juice
2 tablespoons extra-virgin olive oil
Salt and freshly ground pepper
½ pound carrots, cut into thin matchsticks
¼ cup chopped cilantro or parsley
2 tablespoons chopped mint

Smash the garlic with the flat of a knife. Transfer it to a small bowl, and add the cumin, coriander, crushed red pepper, and lemon juice, and then whisk in the olive oil. Season the dressing with salt and pepper.

Put the carrots in a large bowl, and toss them with the dressing, cilantro, and mint.

Picnic Carrots

Pack these up for your next picnic, or take them to the lake for the weekend. They taste better over time and perk up a cheese plate or a backyard barbecue.

½ **pound carrots, cut into 4 × ½-inch sticks**
¾ **cup water**
½ **cup cider vinegar**
2 tablespoons sugar
1 clove garlic, crushed
1 tablespoon dill seeds
1 tablespoon salt

Bring a medium pot of water to a boil, and blanch the carrots until they're bright orange, about 1 minute. Drain, and then refresh the carrots under cold water. Transfer the carrots to a bowl.

In a small saucepan, bring the water, vinegar, sugar, garlic, dill seed, and salt to a boil. Reduce the heat, and simmer for 2 minutes. Pour the hot liquid over the carrots, and let the carrots cool, uncovered. Chill in the refrigerator before serving.

Cauliflower

Mounds of golden, purple, and light-green cauliflower brighten the market tables come late July through fall. The newcomer, Romanesco, a pale-green cauliflower from Italy, has pointed florets arranged in a striking geometric pattern. Its taste is slightly milder than its paler cousins.

COOK'S NOTE

Cauliflower and broccoli are interchangeable in all recipes. To prepare cauliflower, cut the head in half, remove the core, and break the florets apart. Chop the core to cook with the florets.
1 pound = 1 medium head = 4 to 6 cups cauliflower florets

Quick Ideas

Creamy Cauliflower Soup:
Simmer a head of cauliflower florets and 1 small sliced onion in just enough water to cover until the florets are very tender. Working in batches, purée the cauliflower and return it to the pot. Add just enough additional water (or stock) and half-and-half to make a thick soup. Season with salt, pepper, and a sprinkle of nutmeg, and serve hot.

Cauliflower with Anchovies: Sauté the florets of one head of cauliflower in a little olive oil. Season with salt and pepper, cover, and cook until the cauliflower is very tender. Remove the lid and continue cooking until lightly browned. Stir in one diced anchovy. Toss the cauliflower with pasta, or serve it as a side dish.

Roasted Cauliflower:
Preheat the oven to 400 degrees. Toss the florets of one head of cauliflower with just enough olive oil to lightly coat. Spread the florets on a baking sheet so they don't touch, and sprinkle them with coarse salt. Roast, shaking the pan occasionally, until the cauliflower is golden brown, about 15 to 20 minutes. Serve with a wedge of lemon.

Cauliflower with Indian Spices

Serves 4

This aromatic side dish is great with grilled lamb. It becomes a light vegetarian supper when served over rice.

1 teaspoon cumin seeds
2 tablespoons vegetable oil, or more as needed
1 small onion, chopped
1 (1¼ to 1½ pound) head cauliflower, broken into florets (about 3 cups)
2 large carrots, cut into ½-inch pieces
Salt and freshly ground pepper
3 cloves garlic, minced
2 teaspoons grated ginger
Large pinch of crushed red pepper

Toast the cumin seeds in a large dry skillet over medium-low heat, stirring occasionally, until you can smell their fragrance, about 4 to 5 minutes (watch that they don't burn). Transfer the seeds to a small bowl.

Return the skillet to medium-high heat, add the oil, and heat until shimmering. Add the onion, stir to coat, and then add the cauliflower and carrots in an even layer. Season the vegetables with salt and pepper, and cook without stirring until the vegetables have begun to turn brown, about 2 to 3 minutes. Stir, and continue sautéing until the cauliflower is tender, another 2 to 3 minutes. Stir in the toasted cumin seeds, garlic, ginger, and crushed red pepper. Cook another minute to blend the flavors. Season with additional salt and pepper, if needed, and serve immediately.

Freezing Vegetables and Fruits

Freezing is the easiest method of preserving the season's harvest.

- Blanch vegetables first: dip them briefly in rapidly boiling water; then drain and refresh them under cold water. Dry the vegetables thoroughly.
- Fruit doesn't need to be blanched. Simply pack it into containers or freezer bags.
- To freeze delicate berries, arrange them in a single layer on a baking sheet and place it in the freezer. Once frozen, transfer the berries to a plastic freezer bag or a container.
- Store vegetables and fruits in heavy-weight, airtight containers or freezer bags. Fill containers to the top; remove as much air as possible from freezer bags.
- Freeze vegetables and fruit at 0 degrees or colder.
- Store frozen fruits and vegetables for no longer than one year.
- For the best texture, eat frozen fruit before it has completely thawed.

Romanesco with Zesty Tomato Sauce

Serves 4

When served whole, pale-green Romanesco makes a stunning presentation. Cut it into wedges to serve.

1 tablespoon olive oil, plus a little more for drizzling
1 medium onion, chopped
3 cloves garlic, smashed
¼ cup pitted and chopped kalamata olives
¼ cup chopped parsley
2 cups canned diced tomatoes with their juices
½ cup red wine vinegar
Generous pinch of crushed red pepper
Salt and freshly ground pepper
1 head Romanesco, outer leaves discarded
2 tablespoons shredded Parmesan

Choose a pot that will fit the whole Romanesco head with about an inch of free space surrounding it. Heat the olive oil in the pot, and sauté the onions and garlic over medium until the onion is translucent, about 5 minutes. Add the olives, parsley, tomatoes, vinegar, crushed red pepper, and salt and pepper to taste. Stir and simmer for 3 minutes.

Set the Romanesco, bottom down, in the sauce and drizzle it with a little oil. Reduce the heat to a simmer, cover, and cook for about 10 minutes. Spoon some of the sauce over the Romanesco, cover the pot again, and continue cooking until the Romanesco is tender, about another 5 to 10 minutes.

To serve, remove the Romanesco and cut it in quarters. Serve it with some of the sauce spooned over the top and a sprinkling of Parmesan.

Romanesco is a delicate, tender, mild-tasting cauliflower.

Celeriac (Celery Root)

Don't be put off by this knobby, gnarled brown root: just taste the dense, ivory colored, nutty beauty within. Celery's ugly cousin is a favorite of the French, who bake it into smooth, sweet gratins, steam and purée it, and shred it for salads.

COOK'S NOTE

Use a sharp paring knife to peel celeriac and trim away the fibrous roots. Once it's peeled and sliced, it will discolor quickly, so hold it in water that contains a splash of lemon juice or vinegar (about 1 tablespoon of acid to 1 cup of water).

1 pound = 2 cups shredded or 3 cups chopped celeriac

Quick Ideas

Quick Slaw: Peel and cut the root into thin strips (about ½ inch thick) and toss with a simple vinaigrette. Marinate for at least 1 hour before serving. It will keep several days in the refrigerator.

Celeriac Apple Salad: Peel and cut the celeriac and 1 large tart apple into 1-inch chunks. Toss with just enough mayonnaise to coat, and season with a splash of apple cider vinegar, chopped sage, salt, and pepper. Garnish with toasted walnuts.

Celeriac and Potato Mash: Peel and cut the celeriac and several large potatoes, and put them in a large saucepan with just enough water to cover. Bring to a boil, reduce the heat, and simmer until the potatoes and the celeriac are very tender. Drain off half of the water, and mash the vegetables together, adding a little cream or whole milk to create the desired consistency. Season with salt, pepper, and a sprinkling of nutmeg.

CELERIAC

Celeriac Gratin

Serves 4 to 6

This rich, gooey potato dish cries out for a green salad and a glass of dark, sharp beer. Since the potatoes and celeriac are baked without cream, you end up with a very pure flavor, enriched by the cheese.

1 whole celeriac
1 teaspoon white vinegar
2 large potatoes
2 cups grated Gruyère
Salt and freshly ground pepper
1 cup vegetable or chicken stock

Preheat the oven to 350 degrees. Butter a 1½- to 2-quart casserole dish.

Peel and cut the celeriac into ⅛-inch slices. Place it in a bowl with enough water to just cover, and add the vinegar. Peel the potatoes, and slice them into ⅛-inch slices. Set aside ¼ cup of the cheese.

Drain the celeriac, and layer the slices in the casserole dish with the potatoes and the cheese, sprinkling with just a little salt and pepper over each layer, and finishing with a layer of cheese. Add the stock. Cover the casserole with a lid or aluminum foil. Bake until the vegetables are very tender, about 45 minutes. Uncover the casserole, sprinkle with the reserved cheese, and continue baking until the cheese is melted and bubbly, about 10 to 15 minutes.

Celeriac and Apple Soup

Serves 4

This soup pairs two ingredients basic to the fall market basket. It gets its lush texture from potato, not heavy cream. The licorice notes of celeriac and sweet, tart apple prove, once again, that what grows in the same season goes well together in soup.

1 whole celeriac
1 teaspoon white vinegar
2 tablespoons unsalted butter
½ cup chopped onion
2 teaspoons chopped thyme
1 small bay leaf
Salt and freshly ground pepper
2 tart apples, such as Haralson, Cortland, or Zestar, peeled and cut into 2-inch pieces
1 large potato, peeled and cut into 2-inch pieces
½ cup apple cider
½ cup water
2 tablespoons applejack or brandy (optional)
Sour cream or crème fraîche
Chopped fresh parsley

Peel the celeriac, cut it into 2-inch cubes, and put it in a bowl with enough cold water to cover and the vinegar.

In a heavy pot set over medium heat, melt the butter and cook the onion, thyme, and bay leaf with a little salt and pepper until the onion is soft, about 10 minutes.

Drain the celeriac, and add it to the pot along with the apples, potato, apple cider, water, and a pinch of salt. Increase the heat, and bring the liquid to a boil. Reduce the heat to low, and simmer, uncovered, until the potatoes and celeriac are very soft, 10 to 15 minutes.

Working in batches, purée the soup in a blender. Return the soup to the pot, and reheat it. If necessary, thin the soup with a little more cider or water, and season it with salt, pepper, and a splash of applejack. Ladle the soup into bowls, and garnish it with sour cream and parsley. Serve right away.

Chard

There doesn't seem to be anyone who knows how this broad, dark-green, leafy plant came by the name Swiss chard. Like kale, chard grows with abandon here. Second to spinach in vitamin and mineral content, its leaves and stems are nutritious (high in vitamins K, A, C, and E and in iron and potassium). Chard is also noteworthy for its ability to regulate blood sugar.

COOK'S NOTE

Chard stems and leaf veins are often removed and cooked separately from the quick-cooking leaves.

1 pound = 5 to 6 cups packed chard leaves and ribs

Quick Idea

Slow-Braised Chard: Remove the stems and thick veins from the chard leaves. Rinse the leaves with cold water, but do not thoroughly dry them. Film a deep sauté pan with olive oil, and add a handful of leaves with several cloves of peeled whole garlic. Set the pan over low heat, and cook until the leaves wilt, about 2 to 3 minutes. Add another handful of leaves, stir, and continue cooking, adding more leaves as the previous batch cooks down. Once all of the leaves are wilted, continue cooking, stirring occasionally, until the water has evaporated and the chard is very tender. Season with salt, pepper, and a splash of cider vinegar.

Chard with Garlic, Dried Cranberries, and Sunflower Seeds

Serves 2 to 4

If you are not growing chard yourself, the farmers market is the best choice. By the time chard gets to the grocery store from a thousand miles away, it's lost its nutritional value and its oomph. Local farmers grow rainbows of chard whose bright-colored stems are reason enough to buy bundles.

1 pound chard
1 tablespoon sunflower oil or vegetable oil
2 cloves garlic, smashed
Pinch of crushed red pepper
½ cup dried cranberries or raisins, plumped in hot water and drained
½ cup toasted sunflower seeds
Salt and freshly ground pepper

Remove the stems and ribs from the chard leaves, cut the leaves into ½-inch strips, and rinse them in cold water, but do not dry them. Heat a large skillet over medium-high. Add the oil, and then toss in the garlic, crushed red pepper, and chard. Sauté, stirring, until the leaves are well wilted, about 3 to 5 minutes. Stir in the dried cranberries, toss in the sunflower seeds, and season with salt and pepper to taste.

Hearty Chard and Chickpea Stew

Serves 6 to 8

This stew uses chard in proportion to the chickpeas for a substantial, pretty dish that incorporates both the chard leaves and the multicolored stems. It's a vegan entree, an omnivore's delight.

STEW:

1 tablespoon olive oil

1 small celeriac, diced, or 1 stalk celery with leaves, diced

1 small yellow onion, chopped

4 cloves garlic, minced

3 cups cooked chickpeas, with liquid

1 pound chard, stems and ribs removed and chopped, leaves sliced ½-inch wide

Salt and freshly ground pepper

2 tablespoons chopped parsley

1 tablespoon chopped thyme

CROUTONS:

6 slices ciabatta or rustic bread

Olive oil

Preheat the oven to 350 degrees.

Heat the oil in a large skillet set over medium-high heat. Add the celeriac and onion, and cook until the vegetables are soft and the onion is translucent, about 5 minutes.

Add the garlic, the chickpeas with their liquid, and the chard leaves and stems. Lower the heat, and simmer, stirring occasionally, until the chard is tender, about 10 minutes.

Meanwhile, make the croutons. Drizzle the slices of bread with a little oil, and toast them in the preheated oven until they are nicely browned. Remove.

Season the stew with salt and pepper, and add a little water or wine if needed. Stir in the parsley and thyme. Serve topped with the croutons.

Chicories

Chicory covers a broad category of bitter leaves—Belgian or French endive (pearly white, tightly packed heads), radicchio (small, tight red leaves), curly endive or frisée (wild lacy leaves). None of these grow easily in our climate, but occasionally you'll find them at the farmers market. Their bitter nature partners nicely with rich foods.

COOK'S NOTE

To prepare any variety of chicory, separate, rinse, and dry the leaves, and discard the tough stems. All chicories will take to braising; they work well in salads too.

1 pound = 8 cups shredded chicory leaves

Quick Ideas

Stuffed Belgian Endive Leaves: Use the broad, scooped leaves to serve smoked fish and spreads.

Chopped Salads: The peppery bite of chopped chicory leaves complements salads with creamy dressings (chicken, egg, turkey).

Braised Radicchio or Escarole: Heat several tablespoons of olive oil in a large skillet over medium heat. Add several cups of chopped radicchio or escarole, stirring and turning until it turns light brown. Add a little wine or water, cover, and cook until the leaves are tender, about 10 minutes. Season with lemon juice, salt, and pepper.

Chicory or Belgian Endive Salad with Apples and Gruyère

Serves 4 to 6

3 heads Belgian endive or one head frisée, cut into bite-size pieces
½ pound Gruyère, diced into ½-inch pieces
1 small red onion, minced
1 carrot, diced
1 stalk celery, diced
2 medium tart apples, peeled, cored, and cut into ½-inch dice
¼ cup Essential Vinaigrette (page 262)
¼ cup toasted walnuts, chopped (page 265)

In a large bowl, toss together the Belgian endive, Gruyère, onion, carrot, celery, and apples. Toss with just enough vinaigrette to lightly coat the salad. Garnish with toasted walnuts just before serving.

Grilled Radicchio

Serves 4

The Italians grill all of their endives to caramelize them and temper their bite. This simple dish also works with endive and makes a fine side to grilled fish or chicken.

2 heads radicchio
¼ cup olive oil
Coarse salt
2 tablespoons balsamic vinegar
1 clove garlic, chopped
¼ teaspoon Dijon mustard, or more to taste
Salt and freshly ground pepper
Grated pecorino or Asiago

Remove any dead or damaged leaves from the radicchio heads, and cut them into quarters so that each section is held together by its stem.

Prepare the grill for high heat. Brush the radicchio with a little of the oil, and sprinkle it with a little salt. Grill over high heat, uncovered, until the radicchio is just charred. Remove.

In a large bowl, whisk together the remaining oil, vinegar, garlic, and mustard.

Toss the radicchio quarters with the dressing. Season to taste with salt and pepper, and sprinkle with cheese. Serve warm or at room temperature.

Collards

Collards are pleasingly humble yet vibrant and big flavored. The leaves are wide and soft. Collards are loaded with nutrients (especially vitamins A, C, and K, folic acid, iron, calcium, and fiber). Most associated with southern cooking, collards sure like the northern climate and soil.

COOK'S NOTE

Collards are a little milder than kale and chard. To prepare the greens, wash them thoroughly and remove the tough stems.

1 pound = 7 to 8 cups collard leaves

Quick Ideas

Southern Collards with Bacon: Wash and chop the greens, but do not dry them; they should be wet when you add them to the pot. Sauté several pieces of chopped bacon in a large pot. Use a slotted spoon to remove the bacon and set it on a paper towel to drain.

Lower the heat under the pot, and add the collards a handful at a time, stirring until they have wilted before adding the next handful. Cover, and cook over low heat, stirring occasionally, until the greens are very silky, about 15 to 20 minutes. Sprinkle with the bacon before serving.

Sautéed Collards with Garlic: In a large skillet, sauté the garlic in a little olive oil, and then add enough chopped collard leaves to fill the pan. Cook, stirring, over low heat until the collards are wilted. Season with balsamic vinegar, sherry vinegar, or red wine vinegar before serving.

Bean and Collard Soup

Serves 4 to 6

This assertive soup bridges late summer to chilly fall. Look for local white beans or pinto beans when at market; they will be fresher and take less time to cook than those that are fully dried. For a heartier dish, add browned sausage or ham several minutes before serving.

2 cups chicken stock or vegetable stock (page 264)
2 cups water
1 cup lentils, rinsed
1 large onion, chopped
1 carrot, chopped
1 tablespoon olive oil or vegetable oil
¼ cup chopped shallots
2 cloves garlic, crushed
4 cup chopped collards
Several dashes Tabasco sauce
Salt and freshly ground pepper
Cider vinegar
¼ cup shredded cheddar

In a large pot set over medium-high heat, bring the stock and water to a boil, add the lentils, onion, and carrot, and simmer, partially covered, for about 30 minutes.

In a large skillet, heat the oil and cook the shallots and garlic until they soften, about 3 minutes; then scrape them into the pot with the lentils. Add the collards, and simmer, partially covered, for 20 to 30 minutes. Season to taste with Tabasco, salt, pepper, and vinegar. Serve garnished with shredded cheddar.

Corn

Sweet corn blasts its way into our kitchens with summer's heat. By early September, I seek more ways to enjoy it off the cob. Our markets offer a range of organic and heirloom varieties such as Ruby Jewel, Sugar Pearl, Brocade, Painted Mountain—each sweet and different. Any corn picked and eaten on the same day will be the best you've ever had, guaranteed.

COOK'S NOTE

After you've enjoyed the kernels, put the cobs in a pot and cover them with cold water. Bring the water to a boil, and then reduce it to a simmer to make a delicate corn stock.

To cut kernels from the cob, cut the ear of corn in half crosswise. This gives you a flat surface and helps keep the kernels from bouncing away. Stand the corn on the cut end, and slice down the length of the ear, cutting between the kernels and the cob (get close to the cob, but be careful not to cut off those hard, tough bits). Rotate the cob and repeat until all the kernels are cut off.

To freeze corn kernels, blanch the kernels in boiling water for about 1 to 2 minutes. Drain and cool; then place the kernels in a single layer on a baking sheet to freeze. Transfer the frozen kernels into an airtight container or a plastic freezer bag, and store in the freezer for up to three months.

1 medium ear = $^3/_4$ cup corn kernels

Quick Ideas

Roasted Corn: Heat a grill to medium heat. Peel back the husks, remove the silk, and then smooth the husks back over the cobs. Soak the corn in water, and then place it on the grill. Grill, rotating occasionally, until the kernels are tender, about 10 to 15 minutes. Serve in the husk.

Quick Succotash: In a deep skillet, melt some butter and gently sauté $^1/_2$ cup of chopped onion, 1 cup of corn kernels, $^1/_4$ cup of chopped green onions, and $^1/_2$ cup of chopped green beans. Cover, and steam until the corn has lost its starchiness and the beans are tender-crisp, about 5 to 7 minutes. Add a little fresh lemon juice and a lot of chopped basil.

Super Fresh Corn Salad: Make this with seriously fresh corn. Cut the kernels from the cob, catching the milky juices in a small bowl as you do. Put the kernels and the corn milk in a larger bowl. Add a little chopped red onion, chopped red bell pepper, chopped mint, and chopped basil. Toss the salad with a little olive oil, lemon juice, salt, and pepper. You can serve this right away.

Quick Corn Toss

Serves 4 to 6

Bright and full-flavored, this is an ideal summertime sauté. Corn and peppers dance in the pan for just a moment; the quick heat draws forth their sweet, hot flavors without dulling their crisp textures. Get it to the table, ASAP.

2 tablespoons olive oil
½ cup chopped red onion
1 small red bell pepper, seeded and chopped
6 to 8 ears of corn, shucked
Salt and freshly ground pepper
¼ cup thinly sliced basil

Cut the kernels from the cobs (page 113). Then stand the ears upright on a plate or in a shallow bowl and scrape a spoon or the back of a knife down each row to remove the remaining pulp and juices, leaving behind the kernel skins. You should have between 3 and 4 cups of kernels and juice.

In a large skillet, heat the olive oil and sauté the onion until it's soft, about 5 minutes. Stir in the pepper, and sauté until it softens, about 3 to 5 minutes. Add the corn, season with salt and pepper, and continue to cook, stirring, until the corn loses its starchiness, about 5 minutes. Season the corn with the basil and more salt and pepper, if needed.

Fresh Corn Soup with Cherry Tomatoes

Serves 4

Rich with the flavors of sweet corn and tangy tomatoes, this intense soup pulls the summer garden into a bowl. It's delicious warm or at room temperature.

6 to 8 ears fresh corn, shucked
10 sprigs thyme
1 small bay leaf
2 tablespoons unsalted butter
1 cup chopped onion
Salt and freshly ground pepper
1 pint cherry tomatoes, diced
¼ cup chopped basil

Cut the kernels from the cobs (page 113). Then stand the ears upright on a plate or in a shallow bowl and scrape a spoon or the back of a knife down each row to remove the remaining pulp and milk, leaving behind the kernel skins. You should have between 3 and 4 cups of kernels and liquid.

Put the cobs, thyme, and bay leaf in a large saucepan or soup pot, and add just enough water to cover the corn. Bring to a boil, reduce the heat, and simmer, uncovered, for about 15 minutes. Remove and discard the cobs.

Melt the butter in a large heavy saucepan over medium heat. Add the onions, season with a little salt and pepper, and cook, covered, until the onion is soft, about 5 minutes. Stir in the corn kernels and their juices. Add enough of the corn stock to cover the corn, and bring it to a simmer. Cook until the corn is very tender, about 20 minutes.

Purée the corn in batches in a blender. If you prefer a smooth soup, strain the soup through a sieve before pouring the soup back into the pot. Taste, and adjust the seasonings. Stir in the cherry tomatoes and fresh basil, and serve warm or at room temperature.

Cheddar Corn Pudding

Serves 4 to 6

Lighter and fresher tasting than traditional corn puddings, this one is ready in minutes. It makes a great side dish and a fine vegetarian meal.

6 to 8 ears of corn, shucked
2 tablespoons unsalted butter
Salt and freshly ground pepper
1 tablespoon thyme leaves
¼ cup shredded cheddar

Cut the kernels from the cobs (page 113). Then stand the ears upright on a plate or in a shallow bowl and scrape a spoon or the back of a knife down each row to remove all of the pulp and milk, leaving behind the kernel skins. You should have between 3 and 4 cups of kernels and liquid.

Melt the butter in a medium saucepan set over medium heat. Add the kernels, corn pulp, and milk plus a sprinkle of salt and pepper. Cook, stirring often, until the liquid reduces by about half and the consistency is thick, about 8 minutes. Stir in the thyme and cheese, and adjust the seasonings as needed. Serve immediately.

Fresh Corn Brûlé

Serves 8

Oh, sunny summer indulgence: corn for dessert!

2 to 3 ears of corn, shucked
3 tablespoons unsalted butter
2 cups heavy cream
2 cups whole milk
8 egg yolks
1 cup sugar
½ cup brown sugar or maple sugar
1 cup blueberries or raspberries

Preheat the oven to 300 degrees. Lightly butter a 2-quart casserole or eight 1-cup ramekins.

Cut the kernels from the cob (page 113). Then stand the ears upright on a plate or in a shallow bowl and scrape a spoon or the back of a knife down each row to remove the remaining pulp and milk, leaving behind the kernel skins. You should have about 1½ to 2 cups of pulp and milk.

Melt the butter in a large skillet over medium-high heat, and sauté the corn kernels until they are just browned, about 6 to 8 minutes.

In a medium saucepan, heat the cream, milk, and half of the sautéed corn, stirring, until the milk just comes to a boil. Remove the pan from the heat immediately. Purée the mixture with the corn pulp and corn milk in a blender.

Bring a kettle of water to a boil.

Meanwhile, whisk the egg yolks with the granulated sugar in a large bowl. Then whisk in the puréed corn mixture and the remaining sautéed corn kernels. Pour this into the prepared casserole or ramekins. Set the casserole or ramekins in a large baking pan, and add enough boiling water to reach halfway up the sides of the ramekins or casserole. Place the pan in the oven, and bake until a knife inserted in the center comes up clean and the custard shimmies when touched, about 30 to 35 minutes for ramekins and 45 to 50 minutes for a casserole. Remove from the water bath, and let cool at least 15 minutes. Cover the custard with plastic, and refrigerate it until you are ready to serve (up to a day).

Before serving, sprinkle the custard with brown sugar and run it under a broiler until the sugar has melted and created a crust, about 2 minutes. Or brown the sugar with a blowtorch. Serve garnished with fresh berries.

Old-Fashioned Corn Relish

Makes about 6 pints

There is nothing antiquated or unnecessary about putting up corn relish, for there is no better way to capture the essence of truly fresh corn to enjoy through the winter. In this version, a red chili pepper heats things up.

4 cups cider vinegar
1 cup sugar
2 tablespoons salt
9 cups corn kernels
3 cups diced red bell pepper
1 cup diced green bell pepper
1 small medium-hot red chili pepper, seeded and diced
1 cup diced carrot
1 cup diced celery
1 cup finely chopped onion
2 tablespoons mustard seeds
2 teaspoons turmeric

Prepare a stockpot or canner and jars (see page 51).

In a large stainless-steel saucepan, stir together the vinegar, sugar, and salt. Bring it to a boil over high heat, stirring to dissolve the sugar, and then slowly add the corn, bell peppers, chili pepper, carrot, celery, and onion; then stir in the mustard seeds and turmeric. Turn off the heat, and let the mixture sit for a few minutes.

Ladle the relish into hot, sterilized jars, leaving ½ inch of headspace. Wipe the jar rims, center the lids on the jars, and screw on the bands until they are just finger tight.

Process the jars for 10 minutes in enough boiling water to cover the jars by 1 inch. Turn off the heat, remove the canner lid, and allow the jars to stand in the hot water for 5 minutes before removing them. Cool the jars for at least 12 hours before storing them in a cool, dark place.

Cucumbers

Cucumbers ask little of the cook: just slice and enjoy. Though they are seldom cooked, a lap around the sauté pan in a little olive oil or butter turns them silky and tender. Exceptionally low in calories (a mere 10 calories per serving), cukes are a nutritional powerhouse, packing potassium, vitamin K, and carotenes into each glossy fruit.

COOK'S NOTE

Most recipes suggest peeling and then seeding a cucumber before use, which is a good idea for large cucumbers or those that have been off the vine a few days. But it isn't always necessary if the cucumber is freshly picked, small, and not heavily seeded and watery.

1 pound = 2 medium cucumbers = 3 cups sliced or diced

Quick Ideas

Sautéed Cucumbers with Lemon: Melt a tablespoon or so of butter in a large saucepan, and sauté about a pound of sliced cucumbers, flipping the slices occasionally, until the cucumbers are tender within, yet still slightly crisp, about 5 to 7 minutes. Season with fresh lemon juice, salt, and freshly ground pepper.

Marinated Cucumbers: Toss cucumber slices with a little rice wine vinegar, a sprinkling of sugar, salt, freshly ground pepper, and chopped cilantro. Let stand for about 10 minutes before refrigerating. Serve well chilled.

Cucumber Water: Steep slices of cucumber in a pitcher of ice water for a clean, refreshing taste.

Cucumber Salad with Feta and Oregano

Serves 4

This refreshing salad should be served icy cold. Look for local feta cheese from a regional dairy, such as Singing Hills Goat Dairy (Nerstrand, Minnesota), to complete this dish.

1 small shallot, minced
2 tablespoons red wine vinegar
6 to 8 small cucumbers
Leaves from 2 sprigs oregano
¼ cup extra-virgin olive oil
Coarse salt and freshly ground pepper
1 ounce crumbled feta (about ¼ cup)

Place the shallot and the vinegar in a small bowl, and set it aside to macerate for a few minutes (this helps soften the shallot's bite).

Peel the cucumbers, cut them in half lengthwise, and scoop out the seeds. Cut them crosswise into slices about ¼ inch thick. (You should have about 4 cups.) Put the cucumber in a bowl, add the oregano leaves, and toss.

Whisk the oil into the red wine vinegar and shallots. Pour the dressing over the cucumbers, season with salt and pepper, and toss. Chill.

Serve the chilled salad on chilled plates. Sprinkle the feta evenly over the salads.

Cooling Cucumber Yogurt Soup

Serves 6

Use smaller, slender cucumbers for this soup; they have a cleaner, livelier taste. Serve the soup in chilled mugs. The soup won't keep, so enjoy it right away.

3 cups strained plain yogurt or Greek-style yogurt
1 cup milk
2 cucumbers, peeled, seeded, and chopped
½ cup chopped red onion
2 scallions, white and green parts chopped
Coarse salt and freshly ground pepper
3 tablespoons chopped dill

Put the yogurt, milk, cucumbers, red onion, and scallions in a food processor or a blender, and purée until almost smooth (leave a few lumps). Pour the soup into a bowl, season with salt and pepper, and chill several hours. Serve garnished with dill.

Cucumber Lemonade

Serves 4 to 6

Refreshing, tart, and simple, this lemonade is best served cold and as soon as it's made. Add a shot of vodka, and serve in a frosted glass with a slice of cucumber.

1 cucumber, peeled and cubed
Juice of 1 lemon
5 cups water
½ cup sugar, or more to taste

Put the cucumber, lemon juice, water, and sugar into a blender and purée. Strain, taste, and add more sugar as needed.

Crunchy Refrigerator Dill Pickles

Makes about 5 pints

Be sure the slices are very thin so they pickle quickly. They'll stay crisp for several months in the refrigerator.

8 cups trimmed and thinly
   sliced pickling cucumbers
2 cups white wine vinegar
   or champagne vinegar
2 cups water
6 tablespoons sea salt
¼ cup sugar
2 teaspoons pickling spice
5 sprigs dill
1 tablespoon dill seeds
1 tablespoon mustard seeds
1 teaspoon peppercorns
5 cloves garlic, smashed

Put the cucumbers in a large glass bowl, and set it aside.

In a medium stainless-steel saucepan, stir together the vinegar, water, salt, sugar, and pickling spice. Bring mixture to a boil over high heat, stir to dissolve the salt and sugar, then reduce the heat and simmer for about 10 minutes. Strain off the spices, and pour the pickling liquid over the cucumber slices. Cover the bowl with waxed paper, and set it aside until cooled to room temperature, about 30 minutes.

Rinse and dry 5 pint jars. Distribute the dill sprigs, dill seeds, mustard seeds, peppercorns, and garlic cloves among the jars. Add cucumber slices to within ½ inch of the jar rim, and ladle in pickling liquid to cover the cucumbers. Leave ½ inch of headspace in each jar. Screw on the lids, and allow the cucumbers to marinate in the refrigerator for at least 2 weeks. Use within 3 months.

Eggplant makes a glorious centerpiece until you are ready to create a pasta or sauté. From left are Sicilian Graffiti and Zebra varieties.

Eggplant

Eggplant is among the most versatile vegetables. Meaty and satisfying, it plays a big role in Indian, Asian, Mediterranean, and Latin American cuisines. Thanks to Hmong growers, we are seeing new varieties of eggplant at the farmers markets each year.

COOK'S NOTE

Eggplant varieties—lavender Asian eggplants, huge deep-purple Italian eggplants, striking white round eggplants, thin Japanese eggplants—are interchangeable in most recipes. The difference in cooking has to do with size and freshness. Peel large or older eggplants, cut the flesh into cubes or slices, toss with coarse salt, and allow to drain in a colander for about a half hour before rinsing and patting dry. This isn't necessary for young, small, fresh eggplant.
1 pound = 1 large or 4 small eggplants = 4 to 5 cups diced

Quick Ideas

Grilled Eggplant: Cut the eggplant into ½-inch slices. Prepare a wood, charcoal, or gas grill. Lightly brush the slices with a little olive oil, and sprinkle them with salt. Grill until browned on both sides, turning once and brushing with additional oil if the eggplant looks dry. To serve, sprinkle with chopped basil and parsley.

Sautéed Eggplant: Peel and cut a large eggplant into small cubes. Film a medium skillet with olive oil, and set it over medium-high heat. Sauté a few garlic cloves, some chopped onion, and the eggplant, stirring constantly, until the eggplant begins to brown. Cover, reduce the heat, and cook until the eggplant is very tender. Serve warm, garnished with chopped parsley and basil.

Baked Eggplant and Tomatoes: Slice one medium eggplant and one large tomato. Layer them in a baking dish, and season with salt, pepper, chopped parsley, chopped basil, and a few chopped kalamata olives. Drizzle generously with olive oil. Cover and bake until the eggplant is very soft, about 35 to 45 minutes. Uncover, sprinkle with grated Parmesan or feta, and continue baking until the cheese is melted, about 10 minutes.

Baba Ghanoush

Serves about 8 to 10

Garlicky and smooth, baba ghanoush is terrific as a dip or a sandwich spread. It will keep about a week in the refrigerator, covered.

1 pound eggplant
2 cloves garlic, minced
2 tablespoons chopped parsley
2 tablespoons chopped cilantro
2 tablespoons tahini
2 tablespoons lemon juice
Salt and freshly ground pepper

Preheat the oven to 450 degrees.

Prick the eggplant all over with a fork and place it on a baking sheet. Bake until the eggplant is very soft when poked with a sharp knife, about 25 to 30 minutes. Remove, and let the eggplant cool.

Cut the eggplant in half lengthwise, drain off any liquid, and scoop the pulp into a food processor or a blender. Add the garlic, parsley, cilantro, tahini, and lemon juice, and process until smooth. Taste, season with salt and pepper, and adjust the seasonings as desired.

Eggplant and Tomato Sandwiches

Serves 2

A hearty slice of grilled or broiled eggplant stands in for the bread in this simple sandwich.

2 (½-inch) slices eggplant
Coarse salt
Extra-virgin olive oil
2 slices mozzarella
2 slices tomato
Salt and freshly ground pepper
Chopped basil

Salt the eggplant slices, and let them drain in a colander for about 30 minutes. Preheat the broiler or heat the grill to high. Dry the eggplant, and brush it on both sides with a little oil. Broil or grill until the eggplant is brown on both sides. Place the cheese and tomatoes on top of the eggplant. Return the sandwiches to the broiler or the grill, and continue cooking until the cheese has melted. Season with salt and pepper, and garnish with basil before serving.

Fennel

Fennel, with its hard, white flesh and clean, licorice bite, is steely and crisp. Like celery, it is tough to grow here. But you will find bulbs that are smaller and more feathery than the large bulbs from warmer climates. It's crunchy and mild when chopped for salads; it turns silky and rich tasting when braised or roasted.

COOK'S NOTE

To prepare fennel, remove the fronds and slice or dice the bulb. The fronds make a pretty garnish, and their licorice taste is a nice addition to stock.

1 pound = 2 large or 4 small bulbs fennel = 2 cups diced

Quick Ideas

Braised Fennel with Olives: Slice a fennel bulb and a small onion into ¼-inch pieces. Film the bottom of a sauté pan with some oil, and set it over medium heat. Sauté the onion and the fennel until they are tender but not overly soft. Add a handful of kalamata olives and a splash of lemon or orange juice, and cook a minute or two. Serve warm or at room temperature.

Fennel and Apple Slaw: Shred equal parts fennel and apple. Toss with just enough good mayonnaise to lightly coat. Serve garnished with toasted chopped walnuts and dried cranberries.

Baked Fennel with Tomatoes and Parmesan: Slice a fennel bulb and a large tomato, and arrange them in a small, shallow baking dish. Cover the vegetables with vegetable stock or chicken stock and a sprinkling of Parmesan. Bake in a preheated 350-degree oven until the stock has been absorbed and the dish is nicely browned. This is delicious with roasted chicken.

Angel Hair Pasta with Fennel and Spicy Tomatoes

Serves 4 to 6

The smaller fennel bulbs at our farmers markets tend to have a more pronounced licorice flavor that pairs nicely with the tang of good tomatoes.

2 tablespoons olive oil or vegetable oil

1 medium onion, chopped

1 large fennel bulb, chopped

5 cloves garlic, minced

2 teaspoons chopped thyme

1 teaspoon fennel seeds, crushed

Generous pinch of crushed red pepper

1 cup dry white wine

6 to 8 medium plum tomatoes, coarsely chopped, or one 28-ounce can
    diced tomatoes with their liquid

1 pound angel hair pasta

¼ cup finely grated Parmesan

½ cup chopped parsley

¼ cup chopped basil

Cook the pasta in a large pot of lightly salted boiling water until it's tender but still firm. Serve the sauce over the pasta, and sprinkle with Parmesan, parsley, and basil.

Heat the oil in a large, deep skillet over medium heat, and add the onion, fennel, garlic, thyme, fennel seeds, and crushed red pepper. Cook, stirring, until the onion is translucent, about 8 to 10 minutes. Stir in the white wine and the tomatoes, reduce the heat, and simmer until the tomatoes are very soft and the liquid is reduced by about half. If the sauce begins to look dry, add a little of the pasta cooking water. Season the sauce with salt and pepper.

Roasted Fennel and Pears

Serves 4 to 6

Roasting caramelizes the fennel and intensifies the sweetness of the pears. This makes a beautiful side dish for pork or chicken.

2 fennel bulbs, trimmed and cut into ½-inch wedges

2 small pears, peeled, cored, and cut into 1-inch wedges

2 tablespoons sunflower oil

Salt and freshly ground pepper

Preheat the oven to 400 degrees.

Toss all of the ingredients together in a large bowl. Spread the fennel and pears in a single layer on a baking sheet, and roast, turning once, until they are golden, about 20 minutes.

Fiddlehead Ferns

The tiny fiddlehead, shaped like the head of a violin, is a young ostrich fern. It is sometimes called poor man's asparagus. If you can't find fiddleheads in the woods, go to the farmers market; they are rarely available in stores.

COOK'S NOTE

To prepare fiddleheads, trim the dark ends from the stem and then soak them in a big bowl of water for a few minutes. Swirl them around to remove any grit or bugs. Pat them dry, rubbing off the last bits of chaff.

1 cup = ½ pound fiddleheads

Quick Idea

Sautéed Fiddleheads: Sauté fiddleheads in a little butter or olive oil. Cover the pan, and cook until the fiddleheads are tender, about 3 to 4 minutes. Serve right away.

Spring Vegetable Frittata with Chèvre

Serves 4 to 6

A frittata, a flat Spanish omelet, is always served at room temperature, never warm. This recipe puts the odds and ends left from a market excursion to good use.

½ pound fiddlehead ferns, cleaned
2 tablespoons unsalted butter
1 small shallot, chopped
1 bunch spring onions, thinly sliced
1 cup spinach
8 eggs
¼ cup chopped Italian parsley
3 tablespoons chopped thyme
Salt and freshly ground pepper
½ cup chèvre

Preheat the oven to 400 degrees.

Put the fiddleheads in a pot with enough water to just cover. Bring to a boil, reduce the heat, and simmer. When the fiddleheads turn brilliant green, about 1 minute, drain and rinse them well.

Melt the butter in a large ovenproof skillet set over medium heat, and lightly sauté the shallots, onions, fiddleheads, and spinach until the spinach is limp, about 1 minute.

Beat the eggs in a large bowl, and then beat in the parsley, thyme, and a little salt and pepper. Pour the eggs over the vegetables in the skillet, and cook over medium-low heat until the bottom of the frittata is firm, about 10 minutes. Sprinkle the cheese on top, and transfer the skillet to the oven.

Bake the frittata, checking it every 5 minutes or so, until the top is no longer runny and the cheese is melted and bubbly, about 10 to 20 minutes. To serve, cut into wedges.

Garlic

Jeff Adelman, "the Herb Man," sells more than fifty varieties of garlic at the St. Paul Farmers Market. The heads fall into two categories:

Softneck garlic has stalks that are soft and pliable. It tends to be strong flavored and stores well. This is the type of garlic that's often braided.

Hardneck garlic has fewer layers of thin, papery skin and is best used quickly while it is still fresh. It doesn't keep long (its cloves tend to turn soft and mushy).

COOK'S NOTE

Store garlic in a cool, dry place, and do not remove the papery skin until ready to use.

Quick Ideas

Roasted Garlic: Slice ¼ inch off the top of a head of garlic. Drizzle in just a little extra-virgin olive oil, and roast in a preheated 350-degree oven for about 45 to 60 minutes. Serve roasted garlic with a roast or alongside toasted baguette slices so guests can squeeze cloves onto the bread.

Fresh Garlic Butter: Finely mince 1 clove of garlic, and mash it and 1 tablespoon of chopped fresh parsley into ¼ cup of softened unsalted butter. Serve on steamed vegetables or crusty bread.

Fresh Garlic Oil: Smash 1 clove of garlic, place it in a glass jar or a small crock, and add about ¼ cup of extra-virgin olive oil. Store covered in the refrigerator to brush on bread before grilling, drizzle over steak as it comes off the grill, and to splash over cooked white beans.

Green Garlic and Garlic Scapes

Green garlic is young garlic harvested before the bulb begins to develop. It is the first real crop of the year, a sure sign of spring. Highly prized in Europe and Asia, its lively flavor enhances stir-fries and soups without overpowering a dish.

Garlic scapes are the tender, immature flower clusters that form on hardneck garlic plants in June. Their flavor is stronger than chives but milder than fresh garlic. Scape season is short: by June's end the stems become woody and the flowers develop. Garlic growers harvest the scapes so the plants will use all of their energy to form larger heads of garlic.

COOK'S NOTE
Use green garlic as you might chives or green onions; be warned, however, that the flavor is stronger.

1 stalk = 1 garlic clove

Quick Ideas

Green Garlic: Snip green garlic to toss over a pizza, mash into potatoes, and stir into rice as it cooks. Toss chopped green garlic into stir-fries and sautés.

Sautéed Garlic Scapes: Sauté garlic scapes in a little butter, and serve them as a side for grilled chicken or steak.

Garlic Scape Pesto: Put a dozen or more garlic scapes, ½ cup of nuts (try pine nuts, almonds, or walnuts), ½ cup of shredded Parmesan, and salt and pepper in a food processer. Purée until the ingredients are finely chopped; then add ½ cup of olive oil in a slow stream and process to a paste.

Real Garlic-Herb Bread

Serves 6

Garlic is one of the most ancient and most important seasonings. In this simple recipe—just bread, butter, herbs—garlic shines. Everyone around will be drawn to the kitchen, starved, by the scent of this bread.

6 cloves garlic, chopped
¼ cup chopped parsley
2 tablespoons marjoram leaves
1 tablespoon thyme leaves
¼ cup good-quality unsalted butter
¼ cup extra-virgin olive oil
Salt and freshly ground pepper
1 large loaf ciabatta

Preheat the oven to 350 degrees.

Put the garlic, parsley, marjoram, and thyme in a food processor fitted with a steel blade. Process the herbs, and then add the butter and oil.

Slice the ciabatta in half lengthwise. Spread the butter mixture on the bottom and top halves of the ciabatta and place them back together. Wrap the bread in aluminum foil, and place it on a sheet pan. Bake the bread for about 5 minutes; then unwrap it and bake another 5 minutes. Slice and serve the bread while it's hot.

Roasted Garlic Soup

Serves 4 to 6

Garlic becomes a much different vegetable when gently and slowly cooked to a caramel brown. In this soup, the mellow nuttiness of garlic comes through loud and clear.

2 heads garlic
2 tablespoons sunflower oil or olive oil
2 bay leaves
2 medium sweet onions, chopped
1 large carrot, minced
1 large potato, peeled and cubed
2 cups chicken stock or vegetable stock (page 264)
½ cup dry white wine
Salt and freshly ground pepper
2 tablespoons crème fraîche or sour cream

Preheat the oven to 350 degrees.

Cut the top off each head of garlic so the tips of the cloves are exposed. Place them in a small ovenproof casserole dish or a sheet of aluminum foil and drizzle with 1 tablespoon of the oil. Set a bay leaf on top of each head, and cover the dish or close the foil around the garlic. Bake until the garlic is very soft, about 45 minutes. Remove from the oven and let cool slightly. Squeeze the garlic heads over a small bowl to release the roasted cloves. Discard the husks and the bay leaves.

In a large, heavy saucepan, heat the remaining oil, add the onions, and cook over medium heat until the onions are translucent, about 5 minutes. Add the carrots, and continue to cook until they soften, about 5 minutes. Stir in the potato, stock, wine, roasted garlic, and salt and pepper to taste. Bring the soup to a boil; then reduce the heat to a simmer and continue cooking, covered, over low until the flavors come together, about 35 minutes.

Purée the soup until smooth using an immersion blender or, working with small batches, in a blender. Return the soup to the saucepan, and whisk in the crème fraîche. Warm the soup without boiling it.

Ginger

Lonny and Sandy Dietz of Whitewater Gardens Farm grow ginger to sell at the Winona farmers market. It's tender and mild, so there's no need to peel it. Ginger is difficult to grow, but the Dietzes nurture it in their geothermal greenhouse, which allows them to extend the season and grow throughout the year, defying our difficult climate.

COOK'S NOTE

If you can't find fresh local ginger, use the roots imported from Hawaii. Peel off the tough skin before chopping the ginger, or simply use a Microplane grater; the tough skin will peel back as you grate the root.

Quick Ideas

Ginger Honey: Gently warm several pieces of ginger in enough honey to cover them. Transfer the honey to a jar, and allow it to cool before covering. Use the honey to sweeten tea or to drizzle over yogurt or cereal.

Ginger Tea: Steep several slices of fresh ginger in enough hot water to cover. Use this concentrate to flavor tea or coffee, or add it to dressing or to Asian stock to bolster its flavor.

Fresh Ginger Sweet Potatoes

Serves 4

2 to 3 large sweet potatoes
2 tablespoons grated ginger
2 tablespoons honey
¼ cup heavy cream, or more as needed
Salt and freshly ground pepper

Preheat the oven to 350 degrees.

Cut an X in each sweet potato, and roast until they are very soft, 45 to 60 minutes. Open the sweet potatoes, and scoop the flesh into a large bowl. Add the ginger, honey, and cream, and mash the potatoes by hand (or use electric beaters to whip the potatoes), adding more cream if necessary. Season with salt and pepper.

Herbs

Herbs grow with abandon in these parts and are available in infinite variety at the markets. This very basic user's guide will get you started, but it's best to ask the farmer for growing and cooking tips. Bonnie Dehn's cookbook (*Herbs in a Minnesota Kitchen*) offers recipes as does her Web site, www. dehnsgardenherbs.com.

Basil: Marvelous basil varieties are offered by Dehn's Garden at the Minneapolis Farmers Market and by the Herb Man at the downtown St. Paul Farmers Market. Heat destroys the flavor of basil, so use it in raw foods or add it just before serving a hot dish. Varieties include:

Anise: licorice aroma
Cinnamon: cinnamon and hints of clove
Fino: intensely aromatic
Genovese: strong basil flavor and scent
Lemon: bright-green leaves with a mild
    lemon note
Opal: purple and milder than green basil
Napolitano: light fragrance and mellow
    flavor

Borage: This plant features light-purple blossoms; the leaves have a mild, cucumber flavor. It's great in salads.

Chervil: These soft, lacy leaves are delicate and taste of licorice and parsley.

Chives: Use chives with abandon wherever onions are called for. Pretty purple chive flowers make lovely garnishes. Garlic chives resemble chives but taste more like garlic.

Cilantro: Cilantro is a staple of Middle Eastern, Indian, Asian, Latin American, Southwestern, and Caribbean cuisines. Cilantro and tomatillos have a natural affinity for each other. These fresh leaves lose their flavor when cooked, so add them to soups, stews, and pasta right before serving.

Dill: Especially good with cucumbers, beets, eggs, and fish, this is the must-have ingredient in dill pickles.

French Tarragon: The long spiky leaves have a bright licorice flavor that works well with chicken, eggs, and salads. It is often used to flavor vinegar.

Lavender: Beautiful blossoms, fragrant leaves, potent flavor! Use sparingly to flavor ice cream, honey, or steak.

Lemongrass: Light-green grass rises out of a scallion-like base. It has a lemony flavor and fragrance, great for flavoring soups, curries, fish dishes, and teas. It is best if peeled and chopped or crushed before use.

Lovage: It looks like a many-leaved celery plant and has a strong, celery-like flavor and aroma. It's wonderful in salads and with chicken.

Marjoram: Oregano's sweeter-tasting sister is wonderful in soups, stews, and tomato sauces.

Mint: Like basil, the number of mint varieties has exploded, giving us wonderful options for salads, fish, poultry, jellies, and, of course, drinks, like the iconic julep. Here's just a small sample of what you'll find (most taste like their names):

    apple mint
    black peppermint (super strong)
    candy (tastes like a Lifesaver)
    chocolate
    doublemint (yes, peppermint and spearmint in one)

Oregano: This is the classic herb in Mediterranean dishes, especially those of Italian and Greek origins. It's classic for seasoning tomato sauce.

Parsley: Use it in everything.

Rosemary: This herb is especially strong and piney tasting. Finely chop the leaves, or, for a lighter flavor, toss a whole branch into soups and stews, and then remove it before serving. Use rosemary branches for basting grilled foods.

Sage: Sage, with its pretty silver-green leaves and musty fragrance, tastes of fall and Thanksgiving turkey. Fry the leaves in a little oil until crisp for a garnish.

Savory: The two varieties, winter and summer, resemble each other, but winter savory tastes more like rosemary and summer savory tastes of oregano. They both work well with roasted vegetables and chicken.

Shiso: The quintessential Japanese herb, shiso's large green or purple leaves taste like mint and lemon and can be just a tad bitter. It's great combined with basil.

Thyme: There are many thyme varieties, but all are aromatic and great with fish, chicken, carrots, and corn.

Verbena: The variety of verbena most often used in cooking is lemon verbena. Its citrusy notes are great in vinaigrettes, sorbet, and dessert sauces.

Basic Pesto

Makes about 1 to 1 ½ cups

Basil is the herb most often associated with pesto. When made with mint, this simple sauce is terrific on grilled vegetables and grilled lamb, tossed with steamed new potatoes, or stirred into the dressing for chicken salad. Try swirling it into chilled gazpacho or vichyssoise right before serving. Note that, unlike pesto made with basil or parsley, mint pesto does not keep more than a day.

2 cups herb leaves (mint, cilantro, basil, lemon balm, or whatever you have)
¼ cup Italian parsley leaves
1 clove garlic
⅓ cup pine nuts
2 to 3 tablespoons lemon juice
¾ cup vegetable oil, or more as needed
Salt and freshly ground pepper

Put the herbs, parsley, garlic, pine nuts, and lemon juice in a food processor fitted with a steel blade. Add about ¼ cup of the oil, and pulse several times. Then, with the motor running, slowly add ½ cup of the oil to make a creamy sauce (add a little more oil, if needed). Add salt and pepper to taste. Use immediately.

Herb Popovers

The fresh herbs in these popovers are a pretty touch. Serve them with herbed butter.

6 large eggs
2 cups milk
6 tablespoons unsalted butter, melted
2 cups all-purpose flour
1 tablespoon finely chopped parsley
1 tablespoon finely chopped mixed herbs (basil, thyme, oregano)
1 teaspoon salt

Preheat the oven to 375 degrees. Generously grease a popover tin or eight 7-ounce ovenproof custard cups, and place them on a baking sheet.

In a large metal bowl, beat the eggs until frothy. Beat in the milk and butter. Then beat in the flour, parsley, herbs, and salt.

Divide the batter among the prepared cups. Bake 1 hour. Using a sharp knife, pierce the side of each popover to allow the steam to escape. Continue baking until browned, about 10 minutes longer. Turn the popovers out of the cups, and serve them immediately.

Fresh Herb Butter

Makes ½ cup

Vary the herbs to create different butters. Herb butters freeze beautifully and are wonderful for finishing off a steak, chicken breast, fish fillet, or vegetables right before serving.

½ cup unsalted butter, softened
2 tablespoons dry white wine
1 tablespoon finely chopped mixed herbs, including thyme, parsley, and basil
½ teaspoon salt, or to taste

In a small bowl, mash the butter with the wine, herbs, and salt until blended. Transfer the butter to a sheet of waxed paper or parchment paper, and roll it into a 6-inch log. Refrigerate for at least 1 hour before using, or freeze.

Jicama

Jicama does grow here, but it takes some work. A native of South America, jicama looks like a big, woody turnip, but its flesh is juicy, crunchy, and sweet. In grocery stores, it's imported as a mature root with a tough skin. Sold fresh from the garden at our farmers markets, jicama has a thin and delicate skin, and the flesh is especially tender.

COOK'S NOTE

Use jicama as you might celery; its crunch adds texture to salads and slaws. It's also great served icy cold as a snack, especially on a blasting hot summer day.

1 pound = 2 to 2 ½ cups chopped jicama

Quick Ideas

Jicama Crisps: Cut jicama into 1 × 2-inch sticks, drench them in lime juice, and sprinkle on some chili powder. Serve icy cold.

Jicama Slaw: Toss shredded jicama into any coleslaw recipe for additional crunch.

Spicy Jicama Slaw

Serves 4

Spiked with chili powder and doused with lime juice, this easy slaw is refreshing on a hot summer day. Serve the slaw icy cold.

1 small jicama, peeled and shredded
1 cup napa cabbage, shredded
1 carrot, shredded
¼ cup fresh lime juice
1 tablespoon ancho chili powder, or to taste
1 tablespoon honey
⅓ cup vegetable oil
Salt and freshly ground pepper
¼ cup finely chopped cilantro

Toss the jicama, cabbage, and carrot together in a medium bowl. In a small bowl, whisk together the lime juice, chili powder, and honey. Continue whisking while adding the oil in a slow, steady stream. Toss the vegetables with the dressing. Season to taste with salt and pepper, and toss in the chopped cilantro. Serve icy cold.

Jicama Watermelon Salad

Serves 4

Jicama and watermelon are natural partners: they're both crunchy and juicy, yet while the watermelon is sweet, the jicama is slightly nutty and bland. Here, they are seasoned with just a drizzle of raspberry vinegar, a little pepper, and chopped mint. Serve this salad on lettuce leaves for a fine, refreshing starter course.

1 small jicama, peeled and cut into 2-inch chunks
2 cups 2-inch watermelon chunks
1 tablespoon raspberry vinegar
2 tablespoons hazelnut oil or olive oil
1 tablespoon chopped basil
Salt and freshly ground pepper

In a medium bowl, toss together the jicama and the watermelon. In a small bowl, whisk together the vinegar with the oil. Toss the jicama and watermelon with the dressing, and then toss in the basil along with some salt and pepper. Serve cold.

Kale

Nothing beats kale. It's a super food—loaded with vitamins and antioxidants—that's also beautiful and delicious. At the market, you'll find bundles of dark green dinosaur kale (named for its size and splendor) and curly kale in shades of green-gray, blue, deep green, purple, and sometimes yellow. Red Russian kale grows late into the season. Early in the spring, kale is tender enough to toss in a salad; come late season, it's lovely braised.

COOK'S NOTE

To prepare kale, remove the tough stem, spine, and ribs that run down the center of the leaves. Like spinach, kale reduces during cooking, so it's best to start with what appears to be a large amount. It will wilt down quickly.

1 pound = 4 to 6 cups sliced leaves

Quick Ideas

Kale Chips: Brush the kale with olive oil, sprinkle on coarse salt, and roast in a preheated 350- or 400-degree oven until crisp, about 5 to 8 minutes.

No-Fail Kale Sauté: Coat a pan with light sesame oil, and sauté kale until it's limp. Remove the pan from the heat, and toss the kale with dark sesame oil and rice wine vinegar. Drizzle with tamari sauce and toasted sesame seeds before serving.

Marinated Kale Salad

Serves 4 to 6

Here, the peppery notes of kale make a nice counter to sweet carrots and dried cranberries. This salad tastes better a day, or even two days, after it's made. The kale's flavor mellows and harmonizes with the rest of the ingredients.

For the best flavor, use a cold-pressed organic sunflower seed oil to make the dressing. Organic sunflower oils from Smude and Driftless Organics are available in natural food co-ops or online.

2 tablespoons sunflower oil
1 tablespoon cider vinegar
1 teaspoon honey
1 pound dinosaur or other kale, stemmed and finely chopped
1 small sweet onion, finely chopped
2 large carrots, shredded
¼ cup dried cranberries or raisins
Salt and freshly ground pepper
¼ cup toasted sunflower seeds

In a large bowl, whisk together the oil, vinegar, and honey. Add the kale, onion, carrots, and dried cranberries and toss to coat. Season with salt and pepper, and sprinkle with the sunflower seeds. This salad keeps nicely, and tastes better the day after it's made.

Braised Dinosaur Kale with Garlic

Serves 4 to 6

This is great as a side dish, but even better on top of a pizza or bruschetta.

2 to 3 tablespoons extra-virgin olive oil
1 large onion, thinly sliced
3 cloves garlic, thinly sliced
2 big bunches (about 2 pounds) dinosaur kale, stemmed and roughly chopped
1 bunch parsley, chopped
Coarse salt and freshly ground pepper

Film a large, heavy skillet with some of the oil, and set it over medium-low heat. Sauté the onion until it is soft but not brown, and then add the garlic, kale, and parsley and sprinkle with a little salt and pepper. Reduce the heat to low, cover the pan, and cook until the vegetables are very soft, about 20 to 25 minutes. Serve seasoned with a little more salt and pepper and a drizzle of olive oil.

Kale and Lentil Soup

Serves 4 to 6

This hearty, satisfying soup helps ease the transition between seasons as winter arrives. It freezes beautifully.

1 cup lentils, rinsed
1 large onion, chopped
2 cups chicken stock or vegetable stock (page 264)
2 cups water
1 tablespoon olive oil or vegetable oil
1 large shallot, chopped
2 cloves garlic, chopped
1 large carrot, chopped
2 large tomatoes, cored and chopped
2 bunches dinosaur or curly kale, stemmed and chopped (about 4 heaping cups)
Several dashes Tabasco sauce
Cider vinegar
¼ cup shredded cheddar cheese

Put the lentils, onion, stock, and water into a large pot and simmer, partially covered, until the lentils are tender, about 15 to 20 minutes. In a large skillet, heat the oil and cook the shallot, garlic, carrot, and tomatoes until they begin to soften, about 3 minutes or so. Stir the vegetables into the lentils along with the kale and simmer, partially covered, for another 10 to 15 minutes. Just before serving, season to taste with Tabasco and a splash of vinegar. Serve topped with cheddar cheese.

Kohlrabi

Peel back kohlrabi's spikes and leaves to reveal a cross between a mild radish and a turnip. Kohlrabi is a farmer's vegetable. It never really became popular in supermarkets, although it's long been a staple at farmers markets. It adds crunch to salads and slaws and is just as good cooked. The smaller, younger bulbs are milder tasting than mature bulbs.

COOK'S NOTE

Remove the spikes and leaves before slicing or dicing the bulb. Some like to include these in cooked dishes, others use only the bulb.

1 pound = 4 medium kohlrabi = 2 to 3 cups diced

Quick Ideas

Kohlrabi Slaw: Shred several medium kohlrabi bulbs, and place them in a colander for several minutes to drain. Shred a carrot and 1 small onion into a bowl. Add the shredded kohlrabi, and then toss with balsamic or red wine vinaigrette to taste. Allow to marinate about 15 minutes before serving.

Smashed Kohlrabi Potatoes: Add 1 or 2 diced kohlrabi to a pot of peeled and cubed potatoes, and bring the water a boil. Cook until the kohlrabi and potatoes are very tender. Drain the vegetables, and then mash them, adding butter and milk as you would for mashed potatoes.

Kohlrabi Slaw in Creamy Cider Dressing

Serves 6 to 8

Don't let the idea of using cream put you off; it gives the salad an elegant finish and softens the kohlrabi's peppery bite.

½ cup heavy cream
2 to 3 tablespoons fresh apple cider
1 tablespoon coarse Dijon mustard
3 tablespoons chopped parsley
Pinch of sugar
2 pounds kohlrabi, peeled and cut into matchsticks

Whisk together the cream, cider, mustard, parsley, and sugar in a medium bowl. Stir in the kohlrabi. Serve garnished with additional parsley.

Braised Apples and Kohlrabi

Serves 4

Kohlrabi, nicknamed the cabbage-turnip, is a member of the cabbage family that is often treated as a turnip. This recipe showcases the best of both the tangy apples and the crisp kohlrabi.

2 tablespoons unsalted butter
1 medium onion, thinly sliced
3 large or 4 small apples, peeled, cored, and thinly sliced
1 bay leaf
Salt and freshly ground pepper
6 medium kohlrabi, peeled and thinly sliced
½ cup chicken stock (page 264), or more as needed

In a large frying pan set over medium heat, melt the butter and add the onion, apples, and bay leaf. Season with salt and a little pepper. Cook, stirring occasionally, until tender and golden, about 6 minutes.

Add the kohlrabi and the chicken stock. Reduce the heat to medium, cover, and cook, stirring occasionally, until the kohlrabi is tender, about 15 to 20 minutes. If the pan starts to dry, add a little more stock. Serve warm.

Ramps, a wild leek variety, are members of the lily family.

Leeks and Ramps

Leeks are members of the lily family, and although they're often treated like onions, they are not related at all. Their flavor is less pronounced than that of shallots or onions.

Ramps are wild leeks and are more assertive than their domesticated counterparts. They resemble dark-green scallions with a skinny bulb and lily-like green leaves. The season for ramps is short, and the plant doesn't store or keep well, so be sure to cash in if you see them at market.

COOK'S NOTE

Use leeks and ramps instead of onions or shallots when making soups and stews.

To prepare leeks, trim the whiskers on the end and then cut them right where the pale green turns darker. Split them lengthwise, and run them under cold water to remove any dirt or grit.

To prepare ramps, trim off the roots and whiskers and any dead layers clinging to the bulbs. Rinse well under running cold water. To cut, stack them so that the bulbs and leaves line up. The entire ramp, bulb and leaves, may then be chopped. Because ramps have a stronger flavor, use about half the amount called for when substituting them for onions.

2 pounds of leeks = 4 cups chopped leeks (white part)

1 pound of ramps = 2 to 3 cups chopped ramps (white part)

Pasta with Ramps and Morels

Serves 4

This dish tastes like spring and the woods after a light rain. The season for morels and ramps is very short, and they don't keep well. You won't find them in supermarkets; they are farmers market specialties.

8 ounces small pasta
1 tablespoon extra-virgin olive oil
1 ounce prosciutto, chopped
1 pound ramps, cleaned and chopped
3 or 4 morel mushrooms,
   cleaned and diced
Salt and freshly ground pepper
¼ cup shredded Parmesan

In a large pot of rapidly boiling, lightly salted water, cook the pasta until it is al dente, or tender, but not too soft. Drain the pasta, reserving about ¼ cup of the pasta cooking water.

Heat the oil in a large, heavy skillet set over low-medium heat, and sauté the prosciutto, ramps, and morels, tossing lightly to coat them in the oil. Cover, and continue cooking until the ramps are soft and the morels are very tender, about 20 to 25 minutes. Add about ¼ cup of the pasta cooking water, and simmer it until it's reduced by half. Toss in the pasta, season with salt and freshly ground pepper, and serve with the shredded Parmesan.

Leeks are marvelous in soups and stews. They are milder than onions and not as bitter as garlic.

Quick Ideas

Scrambled Eggs with Leeks: Sauté a few chopped leeks in just a little butter, add several eggs, and scramble over low heat. Pull from the heat just as the eggs are beginning to firm up, and top with shredded cheese.

Golden Leeks: Film a sauté pan with a little extra-virgin olive oil, and sauté several handfuls of chopped leeks until they are silky and lightly browned. Season them with salt and freshly ground pepper. Toss the sautéed leeks onto pizzas or open-faced sandwiches.

Leek and Potato Soup with Roasted Red Pepper Purée

Serves 4 to 6

2 tablespoons unsalted butter
½ pound leeks, white and light green parts diced
4 medium red potatoes, peeled and diced (about 4 cups)
3 cups chicken stock or vegetable stock (page 264), or more if needed
1 sprig thyme
½ cup heavy cream
Salt and freshly ground pepper
¼ cup chopped roasted red peppers (page 169)

Melt the butter in a soup pot over medium heat. Stir in the leeks, reduce the heat to low, and cook, covered, until the leeks are softened and translucent, about 5 minutes.

Add the potatoes, stock, and thyme. Bring to a simmer and cook, partially covered, until the potatoes are soft enough to mash, about 25 to 30 minutes. Add more stock if it seems to be boiling away too quickly.

Remove the pot from the heat, discard the thyme, and, working carefully, purée the soup in batches in a blender until smooth, adding more liquid if necessary. Transfer the soup back to the pot, and stir in the cream. Season to taste with salt and freshly ground pepper. Serve the soup garnished with the roasted red peppers.

Lettuces and Greens

A few salad greens are treated separately in this book, but those mentioned here are no less distinct. The best time for harvesting any green is in early summer or early fall, when the weather is mild and the temperatures even.

COOK'S NOTE

All of these greens are interchangeable, so don't hesitate to substitute one for the other in any salad calling for greens.

1 pound lettuce = 8 to 10 cups leaves

Quick Ideas

Wraps: Use the leaves to wrap around sliced meats and cheeses or to wrap up tuna, egg, or ham salad.

Pizza: Toss peppery dandelion greens onto pizza or into creamy pasta for added flavor and color.

Butterhead lettuces, such as Boston and Bibb, have small heads and tender, delicate leaves.

Corn salad, a tiny green leaf also called lamb's lettuce and mâche, is nutty and delicate.

Cos, or romaine lettuces, grow erect with large crisp ribs and sharp flavor.

Dandelion greens are best as young, tender leaves; once old, they turn bitter.

Leaf, or open heart lettuces, such as oak leaf, ruby, and salad bowl, have spreading leaf rosettes.

Sorrel, with its long, brilliant green spears that are scalloped along the edges, has a lovely, lemony bite.

Spring Lettuce and Mint Soup

Serves 4 to 6

Use tender, delicate lettuce leaves, such as Boston, plus watercress or sorrel for their peppery bite. Serve the soup piping hot and garnished with peppery croutons for a first course.

2 medium heads Boston lettuce
1 small bunch watercress or sorrel, stemmed
3 to 4 cups vegetable stock (page 264)
1 to 2 tablespoons unsalted butter or extra-virgin olive oil
Squirt of lemon juice or orange juice
Grating of fresh nutmeg
Salt and freshly ground pepper

Shred the lettuce and the watercress. Put the greens and the stock in a saucepan set over low heat, and simmer, covered, until very soft, about 30 minutes. Use an immersion blender to purée the soup, or purée it in a blender in batches, adding butter, lemon juice, nutmeg, and salt and pepper to taste. Return the soup to the stove to warm through. Serve it hot, garnished with croutons.

Chop Chop Salad

Serves 4 to 8

You can make this with any lettuce, but sturdy romaine works best. Accompanied by good cheese and bread, the salad is hearty enough for a main dish, but it also makes a fine starter or side dish.

2 heads romaine lettuce, thinly sliced
¼ cup sliced basil
¼ cup garbanzo beans
¼ cup shredded cheddar
¼ cup thinly sliced salami
¼ cup balsamic vinegar
2 tablespoons good-quality mayonnaise
2 cloves garlic, smashed
¾ cup olive oil
Salt and freshly ground pepper
Sliced cherry tomatoes

In a large bowl, toss together the lettuce, basil, garbanzo beans, cheese, and salami. In a medium bowl, whisk together the vinegar, mayonnaise, and garlic. Whisk continuously while pouring in the oil in a slow, steady stream. Toss the salad with enough of the dressing to lightly coat the ingredients. Season with salt and pepper, and garnish with the tomatoes.

Spring Salad with Asian Dressing

Serves 4 to 6

Early in the spring, the market lettuces are especially delicate and tender—just what we need to brighten up our winter-weary plates. This salad is especially good with lightly sautéed chicken or fish for a light spring meal.

¼ cup rice wine vinegar
1 tablespoon grated ginger
1 tablespoon soy sauce
1 teaspoon honey
3 tablespoons sunflower oil or vegetable oil
6 cups torn lettuce leaves
1 cup arugula leaves

In small bowl, whisk together the vinegar, ginger, soy sauce, and honey. Then whisk in the oil. Dress and toss the greens, and serve them right away.

Shiitake mushrooms are being propagated by several farmers market growers, who also sell kits for you to grow your own.

Mushrooms

"Mushrooms may save the world," Jim Kwitchak, a local mycologist, once claimed. He seemed to understand what researchers are now documenting, that fungi have the capacity to improve an environment contaminated by chemicals. What a delicious idea.

Wild mushrooms may be the last truly wild foraged foods. The best place to hunt them is the forest, but I've had more luck at the market. Not terribly secure in my knowledge of edible fungi, I prefer to leave foraging to the true enthusiasts and professionals who sell their wares through the spring and fall seasons.

If you're inclined to grow your own, seek out the small local companies that sell mushroom kits for shiitake, oyster, and chanterelle mushrooms.

Here's a guide to some of the local mushrooms, fresh from the woods.

Chanterelles: Ranging in hue from pale yellow to vivid orange, chanterelles are in season from September through late frost. They have a lovely nutty flavor and work beautifully sautéed and tossed in pasta, risotto, and soup.

Morel: This is the queen of the forest, the Midwest truffle. Deeply flavored, tasting distinctly of the damp spring woods, morels run from light tan to dark brown with a honeycombed hollow cap and hollow stems. They are so flavorful that you don't need many to enrich a soup, sauté, or stir-fry. I like them best sautéed and served on toast or swirled into softly scrambled eggs.

Oyster: Fan shaped and pale gray, oyster mushrooms are well named. They have a delicate, peppery flavor and are best gently sautéed. These may also be grown from kits.

Porcini, or cèpe: Renowned in Italy, these nutty, buttery mushrooms are available both spring and fall. These resemble our button mushrooms, but with a swollen stem and reddish-orange brown cap. The cap does not have gills, but is spongy and dense. Porcini are deeply flavored, hinting of forest must and fallen leaves. They are also expensive, so use them sparingly to enrich sauces, soups, and pasta.

Shiitake: Light tan to dark brown, shiitake mushrooms feature a dense texture and rich flavor that make them a great addition to meatless entrees. Available year-round, shiitakes are relatively easy to grow from kits.

COOK'S NOTE

Store mushrooms in paper bags or wrapped in toweling, not in plastic, which will trap moisture and hasten spoilage. Do not wash mushrooms until you are ready to use them (they absorb water like a sponge).

The biggest mistakes most people make when cooking mushrooms are to crowd the pan and not cook them long enough. Cook mushrooms until all the water has evaporated and the mushrooms are tender, browned, and flavorful.

1 pound = 2 to 3 cups sliced mushrooms

Quick Ideas

Mushrooms on Toast: Quick rinse and thoroughly dry the mushrooms. Slice and sauté them with a bit of butter, chopped shallots, parsley, and thyme. Season with salt and pepper, and stir in a little wine and some cream. Simmer until the liquid thickens. Serve on a baguette or buttered toast.

Mushrooms Baked in Parchment: Preheat the oven to 450 degrees. Place a variety of sliced mushrooms on a sheet of parchment, drizzle them with olive oil, sprinkle on salt and pepper, and add a sprig of rosemary or thyme. Fold the paper in half; then, beginning at one corner, make small overlapping folds along the edges, and then twist the corners tightly so the package remains closed. Place the packet on a baking sheet, and bake until the steam puffs the package up and the mushrooms are cooked, about 8 to 10 minutes. Serve on top of chicken or toast.

Mushroom and Tofu Miso Soup

Serves 4 to 8

This clear, nourishing soup is satisfying yet light on a cold night. Use a mix of shiitake and white button mushrooms, and any additional vegetables you wish.

1 small onion, thinly sliced
6 to 8 ounces mushrooms, cleaned and sliced
1 small zucchini, sliced into matchsticks
3 carrots, sliced into matchsticks
1 inch ginger, peeled and sliced into matchsticks
¼ cup sweet, white miso, or more to taste
1 cup ½-inch pieces tofu
3 tablespoons chopped fresh cilantro
2 scallions, chopped
Rice wine vinegar

Put the onion, mushrooms, zucchini, carrots, and ginger in a large pot with 2 quarts of water and bring it to a boil. Lower the heat and simmer, uncovered, until the vegetables begin to soften. Whisk in the miso, add the tofu, and simmer the soup for several minutes. Stir in the cilantro and scallions. Season with a splash of rice wine vinegar.

Wild Mushroom Pasta

Serves 4 to 6

This dish is delicious served straight from the pot, or put it in a casserole dish, sprinkle with some cheese, and bake until golden.

1 pound rotini pasta
1 tablespoon olive oil
1 pound wild mushrooms, or a mix of wild and domesticated, cleaned and chopped
1 tablespoon thyme
2 cloves garlic, chopped
1 small onion, chopped
¼ cup wine
¼ cup cream
¼ cup Parmesan
¼ cup chopped parsley
Salt and freshly ground pepper

In a large pot of rapidly boiling, lightly salted water, cook the pasta until it is al dente, or tender, but not too soft. Drain the pasta.

In a large sauté pan, heat the oil over medium, and briefly sauté the mushrooms, thyme, garlic, and onion. Cover, lower the heat, and cook, stirring occasionally, until the mushrooms have released their liquid, about 10 minutes. Remove the lid, and continue cooking until the liquid has evaporated. Add the wine and continue cooking until it is reduced by half. Stir in the cream.

Toss the cooked pasta with the mushroom sauce, Parmesan, and parsley. Season to taste with salt and pepper.

Wild Mushrooms with Barley

Serves 6

The wild mushroom ragout's earthy flavors complement the dense, nutty flavor of barley, a local grain. Local barley is fresher, so it cooks more quickly than barley that has been sitting in a warehouse overseas.

¼ cup unsalted butter
2 ounces pancetta, diced
1 small shallot, diced
2 ounces fresh morels,
   cleaned and chopped
½ pound fresh porcini
½ cup dry white wine
Salt and freshly ground pepper
1 cup barley, rinsed
¼ cup freshly grated Parmesan

In a heavy-bottomed pot or a Dutch oven set over medium heat, melt the butter and sauté the pancetta and the shallots until the shallots are translucent, about 3 to 5 minutes. Add the morels and porcini, and sauté for another 5 minutes. Stir in the wine, and simmer until it is reduced by half. Season with salt and pepper.

In a separate pot, combine the barley and just enough water to cover. Put on a lid, reduce the heat, and simmer until the barley is tender, about 30 to 45 minutes. Serve the mushroom ragout over the barley, sprinkled with the Parmesan.

Morels are the iconic wild mushroom, stalked by foragers throughout the Heartland. When you see morels at market, be sure to stock up.

Okra

Though closely associated with southern fare, okra is making inroads here. It releases an odd, thick liquid that helps thicken soups and stews when cooked for a long time. It's also delicious deep-fried or quickly sautéed.

COOK'S NOTE

To prepare okra, carefully trim around the conical stem attached to the pod and pluck it out with your fingers. Remove any fuzz by running the okra under cold water and gently rubbing it with a paper towel or a vegetable brush. Pat the okra dry with a dish towel.

To prevent okra from becoming slimy in a quick stir-fry or sauté, soak it for 30 minutes in vinegar. Then drain it, rinse it well under cold water, and pat it dry.

1 pound = 4 to 6 cups sliced okra

Quick Ideas

Soy-Glazed Okra: Follow the preparation directions in the Cook's Note. Film a skillet with a little sunflower oil, and sauté the okra for several minutes until soft. Toss with a little soy sauce before serving.

Okra and Tomatoes: Follow the preparation directions in the Cook's Note. Film a skillet with a little sunflower oil, and sauté ½ cup of chopped onions, ½ cup of chopped okra, and ½ cup of chopped tomatoes until the onions are soft. Season to taste with salt, pepper, and a pinch of crushed red pepper. Cover, lower the heat, and simmer until the okra is very soft, about 20 minutes.

Fresh Okra, Corn, and Tomatoes

Serves 4 to 6

This traditional southern dish works beautifully with our local tomatoes

1 pound okra
4 slices bacon
1 medium onion, diced
4 ripe tomatoes, cored and chopped
3 cups fresh corn kernels
Salt and freshly ground pepper
2 tablespoons chopped parsley

About 30 minutes before cooking, soak the okra in vinegar. Rinse it under cold running water and pat it dry. Remove the caps, trim it, and cut it into $\frac{1}{2}$-inch slices.

In a large, heavy skillet set over medium-high heat, cook the bacon until crisp. Remove the bacon to drain on paper towels, but leave the rendered fat in the pan. Set the pan over medium heat, add the onions, and sauté until soft, 2 to 3 minutes. Add the tomatoes and okra, and cook until the okra begins to turn tender, 10 to 12 minutes. Stir in the corn, and season with salt and pepper to taste. Cook until the corn is tender, about 3 to 4 minutes. Serve immediately with the bacon crumbled over top and sprinkle with the parsley.

Onions

Onions are as essential as salt and pepper. They provide a balance of acidity, sweetness, depth, warmth, and body to soups and stews and sautés, so it's wise to use good, fresh, well-cared-for onions from local sources. Too often we take onions for granted, buying those single varieties sold in supermarkets because they store well, not because of their cooking qualities or taste. Our farmers markets offer a wide variety of onions in different stages of harvest. In early spring, the young onions are slender, tender, and mild. Later in the season, when their bulbs have matured, onions are cured in a cool, dry place to develop the papery protective layers. Among the different onions, you'll find soft, sweet Spanish onions that do not store well; hard, crisp golden onions that will keep through the winter; and red onions with a spicy and strong flavor.

COOK'S NOTE

Green onions are small onions that are harvested before they mature. All parts of this long, straight green onion are edible.

Scallions are distinct from green onions, do not have the rounded bulb, and are generally milder.

Spring onions are immature bulbs of larger red or yellow onions. Their flavors are stronger than green onions, yet not as assertive as mature onions.

1 pound = about 1 cup chopped onions

Quick Ideas

Roasted Onions: Peel some small onions, and cut them in half crosswise. Dot the halves with butter, wrap them in aluminum foil, and roast alongside meat or chicken until very tender and golden brown, about 45 minutes to an hour. Remove the foil, and serve alongside the meat.

Grilled Green Onions: Toss a bunch of trimmed green onions with just enough oil to coat. Grill over medium-high heat, turning occasionally, until they are dark gold and very tender, about 5 minutes. Transfer to a plate, and sprinkle with salt before serving.

Crisp, Mild Red Onions: To take the harsh bite out of red onions, soak the slices in ice water for a few minutes before tossing them into a salad.

Onion Confit

Makes about 2 cups

Serve this on bruschetta as an appetizer, or layer it on a savory tart sprinkled with cheese. Onion confit is great tossed with pasta or on top of grilled chicken, steak, and pork. It's slightly sweet and nutty, and will keep about a week in the refrigerator.

4 large onions
4 tablespoons unsalted butter
Salt and pepper
1 tablespoon brown sugar
4 sprigs thyme
2 cups red wine
2 tablespoons red wine vinegar

Peel and slice the onions very thin. Brown the butter in a large, heavy pot and add the onions. Sprinkle the onions with salt and pepper, cover, and cook until the onions begin to soften, about 5 minutes. Stir in the sugar, and cook, covered, a few minutes longer. Add the thyme, red wine, and vinegar, and simmer uncovered until the liquid becomes a thick syrup, about 1 to $1\frac{1}{2}$ hours.

Onion Dip

Makes about $\frac{1}{2}$ cup

Onion dip makes great use of any leftover confit. It's terrific as a spread for sandwiches too.

$\frac{1}{4}$ cup Onion Confit (above)
$\frac{1}{4}$ cup mayonnaise
$\frac{1}{4}$ cup strained plain yogurt or Greek-style yogurt
Salt and freshly ground pepper

Stir all of the ingredients together in a small bowl. Serve with chips, crackers, and vegetables.

Roasted Stuffed Onions

Serves 4

A fine, if humble, supper, this vegetarian entree should be served with plenty of dense, chewy bread to sop up the juices and a tart, crisp salad. Save the parts of the onions you scoop out to make Onion Confit (page 158).

4 large red or yellow onions (about 2 pounds), peeled
2 to 3 tablespoons unsalted butter, melted
1 stalk celery, leaves included, diced
1 clove garlic, minced
1 tablespoon chopped herbs (marjoram, parsley, basil)
6 cups spinach (about 8 ounces), coarsely chopped
½ boule (9-inch round loaf), cut into ½-inch cubes
Salt and freshly ground pepper
¾ to 1 cup vegetable or chicken stock (page 264)
1 cup roasted pecans or hickory nuts

Preheat the oven to 350 degrees.

Slice about ½ inch from the tops of the onions, discard the tops, and trim just enough from the bottom so the onions stand up. Using an ice-cream scooper or a spoon, scoop out the insides of the onions, leaving only the two outer layers. Save the insides of the onions to use in another dish.

Arrange the hollowed-out onions in a baking pan. Add about 1 inch of water, and cover the pan with foil. Bake the onions until tender but not mushy, about 20 to 25 minutes.

Make the stuffing while the onions bake. Melt the butter in a large, deep skillet set over medium-high heat, and sauté the celery and garlic until just softened, about 2 to 3 minutes. Stir in the herbs, spinach, and bread, season with salt and freshly ground pepper, and add just enough stock to moisten the bread.

Remove the pan from the oven, move the onion shells to a work surface, and pour off the water. Fill the onions with stuffing so it mounds out the top, and place them back in the baking pan. Drizzle a little more stock over the onions and bake, uncovered, until heated through, about 25 minutes.

Parsnips

Parsnips haven't gotten the attention they deserve. Most often, they're tossed in with other roots that overwhelm their delicate, sweet flavor. But try featuring them as a side dish or simple soup, and you'll be surprised at how satisfying they can be. They're wonderful in the fall when they're fresh, and even sweeter when left in the ground and harvested in the spring. Good overwintered parsnips are not available in most grocery stores; look for them at farmers markets.

COOK'S NOTE

Parsnips can range dramatically in size from skinny 1-inch diameters to 3- to 4-inch monsters. The great big roots can be woody, so it's best to choose small or medium-sized parsnips. 1 pound = 2 cups chopped parsnips

Quick Ideas

Parsnip Purée: Cook chopped parsnips in enough water to cover until tender, and then drain them. Place them in a food processor fitted with a steel blade, and purée with some butter and salt and pepper. Serve right away.

Savory Parsnip and Apple Sauté: Melt a few tablespoons of butter to film a medium saucepan. Add thinly sliced parsnips to cover the pan in one layer. Cover, and cook over medium-low heat until the parsnips are tender, about 2 to 3 minutes. Core and thinly slice 1 apple. Remove the cover, and stir in the apple slices. Cook until the apple is just tender. Season with fresh chopped thyme, salt, and pepper, and serve right away as a side dish to chicken or pork.

Parmesan-Crusted Parsnips

Serves 4 to 6

These are meant to be a side dish to roast meat, but they hardly ever make it to the table. They're finger-licking good.

1 pound parsnips, cut into inch-thick strips
Vegetable oil or olive oil
Salt and freshly ground pepper
¼ cup grated Parmesan

Preheat the oven to 400 degrees. Line a baking sheet with parchment paper.

In a large bowl, toss the parsnips with just enough oil to lightly coat them, and season with salt and pepper. Spread the parsnips on the baking sheet so the pieces do not touch. Roast the parsnips until tender, about 10 to 15 minutes, shaking the pan occasionally so that they do not stick.

Spread the Parmesan on a plate. Remove the parsnips and toss them with the cheese to lightly coat. Return the parsnips to the oven, and continue roasting until the cheese is melting and slightly browned, about 5 minutes. Serve hot.

Curried Parsnip Soup

Serves 6

This soup is a complete surprise. Coconut milk, not cream, adds richness, so it's satisfying without being overly rich. The seasonings are gentle and warm.

2 tablespoons vegetable oil or coconut oil
1 onion, chopped
1 ½ pounds parsnips, chopped
1 to 2 teaspoons good-quality curry powder
Salt and freshly ground pepper
4 to 5 cups vegetable stock (page 264)
1 cup coconut milk
Juice of 1 lime
Chopped cilantro

In a medium saucepot set over medium, heat the oil and add the onion and parsnips. Cook until their juices are released and the onion becomes translucent, about 5 minutes. Stir in the curry powder and salt and pepper, and cook gently for another 2 minutes.

Add the stock, and bring it to a boil. Reduce the heat, cover, and simmer until the parsnips are very tender, about 30 minutes. Let the soup cool slightly, and purée it in a blender in small batches. Return the soup to the pot, and stir in the coconut milk and lime juice to taste. Warm the soup, and serve it garnished with chopped cilantro.

Peanuts

A staple in the Deep South, peanuts are making their way into gardens here. Roast them right in the shell, sprinkled with a little salt, or shell and use them raw in fiery Asian Peanut Sauce (page 163). The season is short and spotty, so when you find peanuts at the market, be sure to stock up.

COOK'S NOTE

It's best to roast peanuts as soon as you get them, and then store them in a cool, dry area. If kept raw, peanuts may turn moldy or rancid (you'll know if that happens by their smell). Keep raw peanuts in plastic bags in the refrigerator for several weeks; keep roasted peanuts in a cool, dry place, for 2 to 3 weeks.

1 pound peanuts in the shell = 3 to 3 ½ cups shelled peanuts

Quick Ideas

Roasted Peanuts: Spread raw peanuts in the shell in a single layer in a shallow pan. Bake at 325 degrees until they begin to darken and become hot and aromatic, about 20 to 25 minutes.

Boiled Peanuts: This southern specialty is delicious though messy to eat. Add 1 cup of salt to 1 gallon of water, and bring it to a boil. Add one pound of peanuts in their shells, cover the pot, lower the heat to an even boil, and cook the peanuts until the shells are very tender, about 1 to 2 hours; they should be the texture of peas. Drain, shell, and eat warm or at room temperature.

Beer Nuts

Makes 3 to 3 ½ cups

Sweet and salty peanuts, packaged and sold as Beer Nuts, are surprisingly easy to make.

1 pound raw peanuts, shelled
½ cup water
1 cup sugar
1 teaspoon coarse salt, or to taste

Combine the peanuts, water, and sugar in a large, heavy-bottomed skillet set over medium-low heat. Cook until the liquid becomes syrupy, stirring all the while. Lower the heat, and continue to cook, stirring, until the sugar crystallizes, coats the nuts, and begins to turn golden brown. Remove from the heat, keep stirring, and then scrape the nuts into a bowl. Toss with the salt.

Asian Peanut Sauce

Makes 1 cup

This sauce is a keeper: good to keep on hand for dipping vegetables, tossing with noodles, or slathering on a chicken breast as it comes off the grill. It will keep up to 2 weeks, covered, in the refrigerator.

1 cup raw shelled peanuts
1 tablespoon grated ginger
1 clove garlic, minced
1 small chili, seeded and chopped
1 tablespoon soy sauce
2 tablespoons lime juice
1 tablespoon honey
⅓ cup water

In a large skillet, toast the peanuts over medium heat until they are nicely browned, about 5 minutes.

Put the peanuts and the remaining ingredients in a blender or a food processor fitted with a steel blade. Blend or process until the sauce is smooth, adding more water as needed to reach the desired consistency. Taste and adjust the seasonings, adding more honey, soy, ginger, etc., to suit your taste.

Peas

Can there be anything sweeter than peas eaten raw right out of the bag as you're heading back from the market? Whether we're talking about snow peas, English peas, or sugar snaps (a cross of the two), there's no doubt that here's where the farmers market freshness makes a difference.

Snap peas are bright green and crunchy – eat them pod, pea, and all.

COOK'S NOTE

Pea shoots, or vines, are the tender tendrils of the green pea plants, and the best place to find them is at the markets. They are very delicate and won't last long. Use them in stir-fries, or toss them into salads. They're delicious when steeped in a stock (adding a lovely, light sweet pea flavor).

Snow peas and snap peas are grown to eat whole (pod and all). To prepare them, pinch the flower end of the pea pod and pull the string down toward the other end to remove it.

English, or shell, peas need to be released from their pods (which are tough and chewy). Crack the pod at the seam using your thumb; then run it down the inside to release the peas.

1 pound = 1 ½ cups of shelled peas or 2 cups chopped snow or snap peas

Quick Ideas

Minted Pea Sauté: In a skillet set over medium, heat enough oil to film the bottom of the pan. Add 1 chopped shallot and enough peas to fill the pan. Cover the pan, and cook until the peas are tender. Remove from the heat, and toss with a splash of lemon juice and 1 to 2 tablespoons chopped fresh mint.

Simple Pea Slaw: Cut snow or snap peas on a diagonal into very thin slices. Toss with just enough pumpkin seed oil or hazelnut oil to lightly coat, and finish the slaw with a splash of lemon juice or apple cider vinegar. Season with salt and pepper, and serve right away.

Radish and Pea Salad

Serves 4 to 6

A cool salad of sweet peas and peppery radishes, this dish strikes the perfect balance on a hot summer day.

3 tablespoons rice wine vinegar
1 tablespoon honey
1 teaspoon soy sauce
1 teaspoon dark sesame oil
¼ cup vegetable oil
1 pound fresh snap peas, strings removed, sliced into ¼-inch strips
10 radishes, thinly sliced
4 green onions, thinly sliced
4 cups mixed lettuce greens
¼ cup chopped cilantro

In a small bowl, whisk together the vinegar, honey, soy sauce, and sesame oil. Whisk constantly while pouring in the vegetable oil in a slow, steady stream.

Put the peas in a saucepan with just enough water to cover, and bring it to a boil over high heat. Cook just until tender, about 2 to 3 minutes. Drain, and refresh under cold water.

To serve, toss the peas, radishes, and green onions with just enough dressing to lightly coat. Serve on the mixed lettuces, drizzled with additional dressing, if needed, and garnished with chopped cilantro.

Minted Double Pea Soup

Serves 4 to 6

Early to mid-summer is an extraordinary time at the market. Its heady abundance inspired this soup, loaded with two different varieties of peas. Serve it cold on a hot summer eve or warm it gently for lunch on a gray, chilly day.

Shell peas, or English peas, are especially nice when just harvested.

2 tablespoons unsalted butter
1 stalk celery with leaves, chopped
1 small yellow onion, chopped
6 cups chicken stock or vegetable stock (page 264)
1 large russet potato, peeled and diced
3 sprigs thyme
Pinch of grated nutmeg
2 pounds sugar snap peas, chopped
2 pounds English peas, shelled, or
    2 cups frozen peas, thawed
¼ cup chopped Italian parsley
¼ cup heavy cream
2 tablespoons lemon juice
Salt and freshly ground pepper
2 tablespoons chopped mint

In a heavy soup pot over medium heat, melt the butter, add the celery and onion, and sauté until the onion is translucent and the celery is soft, about 5 minutes. Add the stock, potato, thyme, and nutmeg, and bring to a boil. Reduce the heat to medium-low, partially cover the pot, and simmer until the potato is very tender, about 10 minutes.

Add the sugar snap peas, and simmer until tender, about 5 minutes. Add the English peas, and simmer until cooked, 3 to 5 minutes. Stir in the parsley.

Purée the soup in batches in a blender, or purée it in the pot using an immersion blender. Pour the soup through a sieve placed over a bowl resting in a bowl of ice. Stir the soup slowly until it has cooled to room temperature. This will set the color. Stir in the cream, lemon juice, salt, and pepper, and then remove the soup from the ice bath.

If serving the soup warm, return it to the pot and heat through over low heat; do not allow it to boil. If serving the soup cold, cover the bowl and refrigerate until well chilled.

Just before serving, taste and adjust the seasonings, stir in the chopped mint, and ladle the soup into bowls or cups. Garnish with more chopped mint.

Peppers

Peppers evoke a range of tastes, a palette of crisp colors. They are the New World's gift to the Old World. Peppers are categorized as either sweet peppers or chili peppers, but they all begin as green peppers that develop color as they mature on the vine. Here are the categories of peppers you'll find at our farmers markets. Interesting new varieties appear every year.

SWEET PEPPERS

Aconcaua: Yellow and orange, these peppers originated in Argentina and are great fresh, roasted and peeled, stir-fried, and sautéed.

Anaheim Mild: This long, large pepper tastes like a bell pepper, but is thin-skinned. They are often stuffed.

Bell (the most common pepper):

> green: snappy and tart
> red: sweet
> yellow: sweeter than red
> gold: sweet with a little spice
> purple: mild grassy flavor; turns green when cooked
> chocolate: mild and just a little sweet; turns green when cooked

Colorado Mild: This large green or dark-red pepper from New Mexico is most often roasted and peeled.

Cubanelle: A sweet, medium-sized green, red, or yellow pepper, used fresh or roasted.

Holland: This light-purple, white, or yellow pepper is big and conical, with a taste like a sweet bell pepper.

Hungarian Red: This pepper has a distinct smoky flavor. It is used in paprika.

Hungarian Sweet: These long, pointy, yellow wax peppers are delicious stuffed.

Italian Frying Peppers: Slender, conical, and thin-walled, these peppers are light green or red and usually sautéed or stuffed.

Pimientos: These sweet, medium-sized peppers are round with a tapered end. They are darker than red bell peppers and often chopped and pickled or used to stuff green olives.

Sweet Cherry: Round, medium, thin peppers, picked red and green, used fresh and pickled.

Yellow Petite: These sweet, small yellow and red peppers have a fine flavor. They are used fresh in salads and sauces.

Yellow Sweet Wax: Medium-sized, thin, yellow or red, these sweet peppers are often pickled.

CHILI PEPPERS

Chili peppers run the gamut from mild to searing hot. Here's a quick look at the most common varieties:

Anaheim, or California: One of the mildest chilies, long and vivid-green Anaheims are stuffed for chiles rellenos.

Bonda Man Jacques: These hot, lantern-shaped peppers turn golden yellow when they mature.

Bird: Tiny bird peppers are often preserved in vinegar.

Chicken Leg Horn: A Hmong pepper that resembles the back of a chicken's leg. Sold fresh or dried, these are searing and dangerous.

Fresno: About as hot as a jalapeño, the Fresno is short and tapered, hot and spicy. It is red when mature.

Habanero: These very hot peppers, which range from light green to orange when ripe, look like miniature lanterns.

Hot Cherry: It may look like the sweet cherry pepper, but the hot cherry has a kick!

Jalapeño: Thick fleshed and green (and sometimes red), the jalapeño is easy to seed, which reduces its heat.

Mexi-bell: This hybrid of sweet bell and spicy chili peppers is milder than the Anaheim.

Poblano: Mild, dark green (near black) poblanos have a triangular shape. It's hotter than an Anaheim, and a little bitter. When dried, it's called ancho.

Santa Fe Grande: These hot, small, orange-yellow or red peppers are used fresh and pickled.

Serrano: Hot, hot, hot! The green is a lighter shade than the jalapeño; it turns red when it matures.

Yellow Chili: The name covers the Hungarian or Armenian wax, banana, and Caribe peppers. Plump and tapered, pale but spicy, it's an unpredictable pepper. You don't know its heat until you take a taste. (Careful!)

DRIED CHILIES

Dried chilies are often available from the Hmong and Latin American farmers. Look for:

Ancho: The dried poblano is wrinkled and a deep mahogany. It is used in adobo (chicken marinades) and to flavor the dough used to make quesadillas.

Cascabel: The name of this mild red pepper means "little bell." It can be pretty hot.

COOK'S NOTE

The chili's heat is contained in its veins, not in the seeds. Devein and seed chilies before using them. Use gloves to protect your hands while working with chilies, and do not touch your eyes or mouth before you remove your gloves or wash your hands thoroughly. To temper a chili's heat, soak it in water for about 30 minutes before using it.

1 pound = 2 bell peppers or 5 to 8 small chili peppers = 2 cups chopped

Quick Ideas

Roasted Sweet Peppers: Place whole peppers under a broiler or on an open grill, or hold them over a gas flame with tongs. Turn the pepper frequently until the skin is charred and blistered, about 15 to 20 minutes. Place the peppers in a paper bag or wrap them in paper towels for about 5 to 10 minutes to steam, which helps loosen the skins. Using a sharp knife, pull back the skin, cut the peppers, and discard the veins and seeds.

Roasted Pepper Purée: Put some roasted, peeled, and seeded peppers (see above) in a blender or a food processor fitted with a steel blade. Process, adding just a little heavy cream, butter, or olive oil, until the purée reaches the desired consistency. Season it to taste with salt and pepper. Scrape the purée into a jar, and cover it with a slick of olive oil or butter before securing the lid; this will keep for about 3 days. You can also freeze the purée.

Pepper Aioli: In a blender or a food processor fitted with a steel blade, process a clove of garlic, 1 cup of mayonnaise, 3 roasted red pepper (skins and seeds removed), salt, and freshly ground pepper.

Roasted Red Bell Pepper Soup

Serves 4

Roasting red peppers transforms their flavor and texture to be tomatoey, honey sweet, smoky, and lush. In this soup, such qualities shine.

2 tablespoons extra-virgin olive oil
2 onions, chopped
2 cloves garlic, chopped
1 carrot, chopped
1 quart chicken stock or vegetable stock (page 264)
3 large red bell peppers, roasted, peeled, and seeded (page 169)
Salt and freshly ground pepper
Generous pinch of cayenne
Splash of sherry vinegar or balsamic vinegar
Roasted corn or crumbled feta
Chopped basil
Chopped cilantro

Heat the oil in a large soup pot over medium heat. Add the onions, garlic, and carrot, and sauté until soft but not browned, about 15 minutes.

Pour in the stock, and turn the heat to high. Add the roasted peppers and salt, pepper, and cayenne to taste. As soon as the stock comes to a boil, reduce the heat and simmer, uncovered, for 30 minutes, stirring occasionally.

Purée the soup using an immersion blender or a blender. Return the soup to the pot and adjust the seasonings, adding a splash of vinegar to taste. Serve garnished with roasted corn or crumbled feta and chopped basil and cilantro.

Chili con Queso

Serves 6 to 8

Rich and spicy, this gooey, flavorful fondue is great with chips and sliced bell peppers. Leftovers make a terrific filling for grilled cheese sandwiches, or stir them into scrambled eggs.

1 pound Monterey Jack cheese, shredded
2 tablespoons cornstarch
1 clove garlic, crushed
1 tablespoon olive oil
½ cup chopped onion
2 medium tomatoes, chopped
1 small jalapeño, seeded, deveined, and diced
½ cup dry white wine

In a small bowl, combine the cheese with the cornstarch and the garlic. Heat the oil in a medium skillet over medium heat, and sauté the onions, tomatoes, and jalapeño until soft,

Thanks to Mexican, Hmong, and Vietnamese farmers, we now enjoy a range of chilies. Here are thin, red, hot bird peppers; mild green jalapeños; and scorching hot habaneros.

about 1 minute. Stir in the wine, lower the heat, and gradually add the cheese, stirring as you go. Be careful that the mixture does not come to a boil.

Pour into a crock, and serve warm.

Stuffed Chilies

Serves 4

These stuffed chilies are an easy twist on traditional chiles rellenos, comfort food with a kick. The peppers are baked, not fried, for a more expeditious, healthier finish.

1 tablespoon sunflower oil or vegetable oil
1 medium onion, chopped
2 cloves garlic, minced
½ pound ground pork, turkey, or beef
½ cup chopped fresh tomatoes
¼ cup chopped blanched almonds
¼ cup raisins
Salt and freshly ground pepper
4 large Anaheim chilies
Salsa
Sour cream
Chopped cilantro

Preheat the oven to 350 degrees.

Heat the oil in a medium skillet set over medium-high heat, and sauté the onion and garlic until the onion is transparent. Crumble in the meat, and cook until it is no longer pink. Stir in the tomatoes, almonds, and raisins, and season with salt and pepper. Simmer for a few minutes.

Slit the chilies from top to tail, leaving them whole, then devein and seed them. Stuff the chilies with the meat mixture, and set them on a baking sheet. Bake until the chilies are softened and the meat mixture is bubbling, about 25 to 30 minutes.

Serve with salsa, sour cream, and chopped cilantro.

Spicy Sweet Red Pepper Jelly

Makes 5 to 6 half-pints

Pretty jars of this hot stuff make wonderful gifts. The jelly is terrific on sandwiches or alongside roasted or grilled lamb, and makes a fine glaze for grilled or roasted poultry.

3 red bell peppers, seeded and deveined
1 large onion, diced
2 fresh Mexi-bell or hot cherry chili peppers, seeded and deveined
1 tablespoon salt
4 ½ cups sugar
1 ¼ cups white wine vinegar
½ cup lemon juice
1 teaspoon grated lemon zest
1 (6-ounce) bottle liquid pectin or 3 tablespoons powdered pectin

Prepare a stockpot or canner and jars (see page 51).

In a food processor fitted with a steel blade, pulse the peppers, onion, and chilies until coarsely ground. Scrape the vegetables into a strainer, toss them with a generous teaspoon of salt, and let them drain for 3 hours. Press any remaining juices from the vegetables with your hands.

Put the vegetables into a large pot, and stir in the remaining salt, sugar, vinegar, lemon juice, and zest. Bring to a boil, and cook for 10 minutes. Stir in the pectin, and continue boiling for another minute, skimming off any foam with a large spoon.

Ladle the hot mixture into hot, sterilized jars, leaving ½ inch of headspace. Wipe the jar rims, center the lids on the jars, and screw on the bands until they are just finger tight.

Process the jars for 10 minutes in enough boiling water to cover the jars by 1 inch. Turn off the heat, remove the canner lid, and allow the jars to stand in the hot water for 5 minutes before removing them. Cool the jars for at least 12 hours before storing them in a cool, dark place.

Potatoes

Our potatoes are textured, varied, and fabulous, and they fall into three types: firm and waxy, crumbly and floury, and all purpose (in between). Dry-fleshed and floury potatoes cook up to be dry and fluffy and make great mashers, baked potatoes, and French fries. Firm waxy potatoes (red skinned and fingerling) become silky and buttery when cooked, retaining their shape. All-purpose potatoes are great cooked just about any old way.

COOK'S NOTE
Use leftover mashed potatoes to thicken creamy soups and stews.
1 pound = 2 to 3 cups peeled, diced potatoes

Quick Ideas

Mashed Potatoes: Put whole, unpeeled starchy or all-purpose potatoes in a pot, add water to cover, and add a little salt. Cover the pot and bring the water to a boil; then reduce the heat and simmer until the potatoes are tender, about 15 to 30 minutes, depending on the size of the potatoes. Drain. Allow the potatoes to cool, peel them if you wish, and return them to the pot. Add a bit of butter or a little olive oil and enough liquid (stock, milk, potato cooking liquid, or a mixture) to come halfway up the potatoes in the pot. Mash, adding more liquid if necessary, until the potatoes are creamy but retain a few lumps (so diners will know they're homemade).

Stuffed Whole Potatoes: A meal in a peel. Bake large potatoes in a 350-degree oven until tender, about 45 minutes to 1 hour. Slice the potatoes in half lengthwise. Scoop out the potato, leaving the skin intact, and then fill the hollows with chopped cooked vegetables and a sprinkling of cheese. Return the potatoes to the oven, and bake until the cheese is bubbly. Try these other fillings too: sautéed mushrooms and Parmesan; chopped ham, cheese, and parsley; roasted onions.

Skordalia (Greek Mashed Potatoes with Garlic and Olive Oil)

Serves 4 to 6

This traditional Greek dish, a vegan favorite, makes a fine appetizer or a filling for stuffed potatoes.

4 large (about 10 ounce) russet potatoes
Coarse salt
4 cloves garlic, minced
¼ cup lemon juice
1 ½ cups olive oil
Salt and freshly ground pepper

Preheat the oven to 400 degrees.

Prick the potatoes all over, set them on a baking sheet, and bake until tender, about 1 hour.

Holding the hot potatoes with a dish towel, scoop out the pulp into a bowl. Smash in the salt, garlic, lemon juice, and olive oil, adding more oil if needed, and season with salt and pepper. Serve warm.

Potato Salad with Radishes in Lemon Dill Cream

Serves 4 to 6

This potato salad, brightened with radishes and yogurt, is lighter and healthier than salads made with mayonnaise and sour cream. The warm potatoes absorb the vinegar to give them extra punch.

2 pounds small red or Yukon Gold potatoes, scrubbed
Coarse salt
2 tablespoons apple cider vinegar
1 cup sliced radishes (about 7 to 8 small radishes)
3 green onions, trimmed and chopped
2 tablespoons chopped dill
¼ cup strained plain yogurt or Greek-style yogurt
½ cup good-quality mayonnaise
Salt and freshly ground pepper

Put the potatoes in a large pot with enough water to cover by 1 inch. Add a large pinch of salt, set over high heat, and bring to a boil. Reduce the heat, and simmer until the potatoes are tender, about 20 minutes. Drain the potatoes, peel and cut them into 2-inch pieces, and put them in a large bowl. Toss the warm potatoes with the vinegar.

Add the radishes, onions, and dill to the potatoes.

In a small bowl, whisk together the yogurt and mayonnaise. Add the dressing to the vegetables, and toss to coat. Season to taste with more vinegar, salt, and pepper. Serve chilled. This salad will keep for two days.

New Potatoes with Feta and Olives

Serves 4

When you crush a cooked new potato with the back of a fork, it is deliciously receptive to a good, peppery olive oil and a little cheese. This simple recipe makes a terrific vegetarian meal or an easy side dish for a crowd.

16 small new potatoes (Yukon Gold, fingerlings, baby reds, etc.)
3 to 4 tablespoons extra-virgin olive oil
Coarse salt
1 red onion, cut into ¼-inch rounds
6 pitted kalamata olives, chopped
1 tablespoon chopped parsley
2 teaspoons chopped oregano
½ cup crumbled feta
Salt and freshly ground pepper

Preheat the oven to 350 degrees.

Toss the potatoes with just enough oil to lightly coat them, about 1 to 2 tablespoons, and sprinkle with coarse salt. Bake until the potatoes are tender but not too soft, about 25 to 30 minutes. Put the potatoes in a gratin dish, and crush them with the back of a fork.

In a large skillet, heat the remaining oil and sauté the onion slices until they become light brown, about 6 to 10 minutes. Pour the onions and oil over the crushed potatoes, and then toss in the olives, parsley, oregano, and feta, and season with salt and pepper. Put the dish in the oven, and bake until the potatoes are very tender and the cheese is melted, about 10 to 15 minutes.

Radishes

Mid-summer, the market explodes with radishes of all different flavors and shades: Easter egg radishes, tiny and pink; French breakfast radishes, elongated magenta with white tips; daikons, white and up to two feet long. As the season progresses, find big black radishes with inky, rough skin and snowy white, spicy flesh. Look also for the beguiling watermelon radishes (also called red meat and beauty heart radishes) whose pale-green skin covers a rose-colored, mild-tasting interior.

COOK'S NOTE

Radishes add spice to salads and cheese plates all year long.

1 pound = 1 very large daikon, black, or watermelon radish; 6 large radishes; or 12 to 16 tiny radishes

Radish, Cucumber, and Mint Salad

Serves 4 to 6

This salad is the best of midsummer in a bowl. It is peppery, cooling, and tangy. Serve it with a grilled burger or brat.

1 cucumber, peeled, cut in half lengthwise, and seeded
24 radishes, trimmed and quartered
20 cherry tomatoes, halved
¼ cup chopped mint
3 tablespoons extra-virgin olive oil
1 tablespoon cider vinegar
1 teaspoon honey
Salt and freshly ground pepper

Slice the cucumber into ¼-inch pieces, and place them in a medium bowl. Toss in the radishes, tomatoes, and mint.

In a small bowl, whisk together the oil, vinegar, and honey. Toss the vegetables with the dressing. Season with salt and pepper.

Quick Ideas

Radish Sandwich: Lay thin slices of radish on thinly sliced and generously buttered pumpernickel bread.

Daikon Salad: Shred a medium-sized daikon and toss it with just enough dark sesame oil to coat. Season with rice wine vinegar, salt, freshly ground pepper, and chopped cilantro. Serve chilled.

Watercress, Daikon, and Apple Salad with Mustard Vinaigrette

Serves 4

This salad is a favorite of Mai Vang, who trades her daikon radishes for apples from her neighbor's market stall. It is a happy matchup of East and West.

1 large bunch watercress, chopped
1 medium daikon, peeled and chopped
1 large apple (Honeycrisp or Zestar), cored and chopped
1 tablespoon Dijon mustard
1 tablespoon cider vinegar
2 tablespoons apple cider
1 teaspoon honey, or to taste
2 tablespoons sunflower oil
Salt and freshly ground pepper
½ cup toasted sunflower seeds

In a large bowl, toss together the watercress, daikon, and apple. In a small bowl, whisk together the mustard, vinegar, cider, honey, and oil. Toss the vegetables with the dressing. Season with salt and pepper, and sprinkle in the sunflower seeds.

Daikon, an Asian radish, is especially good shredded for garnish.

Rutabagas
$4.00

Rutabagas

Rutabagas are the workhorse of farmhouse cooking. They grow to enormous sizes, store beautifully through the winter, and figure in roasts, purées, and stews. With their pale-orange flesh and spicy turnip flavor, rutabagas add color and zip to dishes made with milder root vegetables.

COOK'S NOTE

Use rutabagas in any recipe calling for turnips; they're milder and bigger and easier to work with. Peel rutabagas before using.

1 pound = 2 cups diced rutabaga

Quick Ideas

Rutabaga Sauté: In a large skillet, melt some butter and sauté cubed rutabaga until it is light brown, about 2 minutes. Add enough liquid (wine, water, stock, cider – alone or in combination) to cover, and shake the pan to keep the vegetables from sticking. Cook until tender and the liquid has evaporated. Sprinkle with salt and freshly ground pepper.

Rutabaga Mash: Cut a rutabaga into chunks, and boil it with the potatoes when making mashed potatoes. The rutabaga will turn the mash a lovely golden color and add a nutty flavor.

Roasted Rutabaga Soup

Serves 4 to 6

You can also make this soup with turnips or a mix of carrots, parsnips, rutabagas and turnips, and you should. But try it with just rutabagas first. The rutabagas caramelize and mellow.

1 ½ rutabagas, peeled and cut into cubes
1 large onion, cut into cubes
3 sprigs thyme
1 tablespoon sunflower oil
Salt and freshly ground pepper
2 cups whole milk
Fried sage leaves

Preheat the oven to 425 degrees.

Toss the rutabagas, onion, and thyme with the oil and ½ teaspoon of salt. Spread the vegetables in a single layer on a large baking sheet. Roast, shaking the pan every 15 minutes so they don't stick, until the vegetables are brown on all sides, about 30 to 40 minutes. Transfer the vegetables to a soup pot. Add ½ cup of water to the roasting pan. Scrape up and reserve the caramelized juices.

Add the milk and the water from the roasting pan to the vegetables. The liquid should cover the vegetables by about an inch, so add a little more water if necessary. Set the pot over high heat, and bring the liquid to a boil. Reduce the heat, cover, and simmer until the rutabagas are very tender, about 20 to 25 minutes.

Transfer the soup in batches to a blender, and process until it is smooth. Return the soup to the pot, and warm it as needed. Season with salt and pepper. Serve the soup garnished with fried sage leaves.

Sweet and Spicy Rutabaga and Root Vegetable Stew

Serves 4 to 6

Satisfying but not heavy, this is just the thing for a vegetarian meal in the heart of winter. Vary the roots to suit your taste and what you have on hand. Peeled and cubed squash works nicely here too.

1 tablespoon extra-virgin olive oil
3 shallots, chopped
1 tablespoon grated ginger
1 parsnip, diced
2 small rutabagas, peeled and diced
1 small sweet potato, peeled and diced
1 fennel bulb, halved, cored, and diced
1 cinnamon stick
Grating of nutmeg
1 cup vegetable stock (page 264), or more if needed
Salt and freshly ground pepper
Apple cider vinegar
Toasted walnuts or hazelnuts

Heat the oil in a large pot set over medium heat, and sauté the shallots and ginger until soft, about 5 minutes. Add the parsnip, rutabagas, sweet potato, fennel, cinnamon stick, nutmeg, and enough stock to just cover the vegetables. Bring to a boil, cover, and reduce the heat to simmer until the vegetables are soft, about 5 to 10 minutes.

Remove the cinnamon stick, and season to taste with salt, pepper, and a splash of vinegar. Serve the stew garnished with toasted nuts.

Spinach

Spinach arrives early in the spring and, through several plantings, lasts well into late fall. If the weather is not too harsh, farmers may harvest spinach as late as December, when the leaves are tough yet remain very sweet. Spinach is loaded with vitamin A, folic acid, and antioxidants.

Spinach grows easily in this region without chemical fertilizers or pesticides. You'll find oodles of great, organic spinach at farmers markets throughout the season.

COOK'S NOTE
Spinach reduces in volume by about three-quarters when cooked.
1 pound = 10 to 12 cups chopped spinach leaves

Quick Ideas

Quick Creamed Spinach: Sauté a pound of cleaned, stemmed spinach and some chopped shallots in a few tablespoons of butter until the spinach is nicely wilted. Lower the heat, and stir in a little cream, grated nutmeg, and salt and pepper. Cook until the spinach is tender, about 1 to 2 minutes.

Spinach Salad: Toss several handfuls of fresh baby spinach with just enough walnut oil or sunflower oil and balsamic vinegar or raspberry vinegar to lightly coat. Toss in sliced strawberries and toasted almonds or walnuts. Serve right away.

Spinach and Gruyère Tart

Serves 4 to 6

This straightforward spinach tart is simple and homey. Serve it for brunch, a light supper, or cut into thin wedges for a starter. It's crustless, so it comes together in a snap. The tart is good served warm or at room temperature.

2 tablespoons butter
¼ cup toasted bread crumbs
1 cup milk
¼ cup strained whole-milk yogurt or Greek-style yogurt
3 eggs
Freshly grated nutmeg
Several dashes Tabasco
8 ounces Gruyère, grated
Salt and freshly ground pepper
1 pound spinach, chopped

Preheat the oven to 400 degrees. Generously butter an 8- or 9-inch-square glass baking dish or a pie pan and sprinkle in the bread crumbs, making sure the bottom and sides are thoroughly coated.

In a medium bowl, whisk together the milk, yogurt, eggs, nutmeg, Tabasco, cheese, and a pinch of salt and pepper. Gently spoon the mixture over the bread crumbs, being careful not to dislodge too many from the pan. Sprinkle the spinach on top. Bake in the preheated oven until the tart is firm, about 30 to 35 minutes.

Spinach Braised with Ginger and Cilantro

Serves 4 to 6

The spinach turns silky when braised. Serve this spicy braise with grilled beef or chicken and rice.

1 pound spinach, stemmed
1 tablespoon sunflower oil or vegetable oil
1 onion, diced
1 teaspoon grated ginger, or more to taste
½ teaspoon ground cumin
1 teaspoon paprika
½ cup chopped cilantro
2 tablespoons chopped mint
Coarse salt
Strained plain yogurt or Greek-style yogurt
Lemon wedges

Rinse the spinach, but do not dry it.

In a large skillet, heat the oil over medium heat and add the onion, ginger, cumin, and paprika. Stir to coat, and cook until the onions start to soften, about 2 minutes. Add the cilantro, mint, and spinach. Sprinkle with salt, cover the pan, and cook until the volume has reduced, about 5 to 10 minutes. Stir, and then reduce the heat and cook slowly for another 20 minutes. Check to be sure nothing is sticking to the bottom of the pot; if it is, add a few drops of water.

When the spinach is tender, serve it garnished with yogurt and lemon wedges.

Spinach Lasagna with Feta and Walnuts

Serves 4 to 6

This layers the classic Greek flavors of spanakopita into an easy-to-assemble lasagna. Leftovers will freeze nicely.

8 ounces lasagna
2 tablespoon olive oil
3 cloves garlic, minced
2 pounds spinach, stemmed and finely chopped
1 cup crumbled feta
1 cup ricotta
2 teaspoons chopped oregano
2 tablespoons chopped parsley
Grated nutmeg
Salt and freshly ground pepper
1 cup walnuts, toasted and chopped (page 265)
6 ounces grated mozzarella
1 cup milk

Preheat the oven to 350 degrees. Generously butter an 8 × 10 or 9 × 13-inch pan and a sheet of aluminum foil large enough to cover the pan.

Bring a large pot of salted water to a boil. Cook the noodles until they are tender but not too soft. Lay the cooked pasta on a platter or the countertop, and cover it with plastic wrap or parchment paper so it doesn't stick.

Heat the oil in a wide skillet, add the garlic and the spinach, and sauté until the spinach is wilted.

In a large bowl, stir together the spinach mixture, feta, ricotta, oregano, parsley, and nutmeg. Season with salt and pepper.

Place a layer of cooked pasta in the baking dish, followed by some of the ricotta filling, a sprinkling of nuts, and shredded mozzarella. Continue layering until you've used up the filling, and finish with the mozzarella. Pour the milk over the lasagna.

Cover the pan loosely with the buttered aluminum foil, and bake until the lasagna is heated through and bubbly, about 30 minutes. Remove the foil and continue baking until the cheese is toasty and bubbly, another 10 minutes or so. Let the lasagna sit for a few minutes before cutting it into squares to serve.

These heirloom red turban squash roast up mild and creamy.

Squash and Pumpkins

It's impossible to buy just one squash. There are too many sizes, shapes, and colors—amber, orange, gold, vermillion, bottle green, lichen gray, cream, and apricot, ribbed and smooth, warty, knobby, big, tiny—and they make a compelling display in the kitchen. Squash flavors vary, but they are interchangeable in all of these recipes. Note that not all pumpkins are edible.

PICKING PUMPKINS

Marvelous looking and perfect for carving into jack-o'-lanterns, field pumpkins make poor eating: they are tough, stringy, and watery. For pies and cakes, look for sugar pumpkins with fine-grained flesh and delicate flavor. Cinderella pumpkins, bright orange in color and squat in shape, make beautiful decorations, containers for soups and stews, and fabulous eating.

COOK'S NOTE

Use any winter squash except spaghetti squash in these recipes.
1 pound = 1 small squash = 2 to 3 cups sliced and diced

Quick Ideas

Toasted Squash or Pumpkin Seeds: Clean the stringy flesh from the seeds and rinse them in water. Dissolve 2 teaspoons of salt in 5 tablespoons of water. Roast the seeds in a preheated 350-degree oven for about 5 minutes, or until they are slightly browned. Sprinkle the salted water over the hot seeds. Stir to coat, and then return the seeds to the oven to dry for a few minutes.

Roast Squash with Apples: Preheat the oven to 350 degrees. Cut an acorn or sweet dumpling squash in half. Scoop out the seeds. Set the squash cut-side up in a baking dish, and fill the opening with apple cider and a few chopped apples. Bake until very tender, about 45 minutes to 1 hour.

Squash with Rosemary and Parmesan

Serves 4

The soft, sweet squash, baked until it collapses into a silky mash, is topped with crisp crumbs, piney rosemary, and sharp Parmesan. The contrast of textures and flavors makes a perfect, warming meal on a foggy, bone-chilling autumn night.

2 medium acorn or sweet dumpling squash, halved and seeded
Salt and freshly ground pepper
4 tablespoons butter
4 tablespoons chopped rosemary
¼ cup dry white wine
2 tablespoons grated Parmesan, plus a little more for garnish
1 cup fresh bread crumbs
2 tablespoons extra-virgin olive oil

Preheat the oven to 400 degrees.

Place the squash cut-side up in a baking dish, and sprinkle it with salt and pepper. Bake until the squash is very tender, about 45 minutes to 1 hour.

Remove the squash from the oven, and scoop most of the flesh into a bowl. Mix in the butter, rosemary, wine, and Parmesan, adding a little more wine to moisten it if necessary. Mound the seasoned squash flesh in the shells. Top it with the bread crumbs, and drizzle the olive oil over top. Return the squash to the oven, and bake until the filling is heated through, the cheese is bubbly, and the bread crumbs are crisped.

Serve garnished with additional Parmesan.

Coconut Curry Winter Squash Soup

Serves 4 to 6

This complex soup is fragrant with warm spices that kindle hunger and draw everyone into the kitchen on a frosty night. The squash is cooked in chunks, not puréed, so its dense, meaty texture shines.

1 tablespoon vegetable oil
1 onion, finely chopped
1 stalk celery with leaves, finely chopped
2 to 3 tablespoons good-quality curry powder
3 cups vegetable stock (page 264)
1 small butternut squash, peeled, seeded, and cut into 1-inch chunks
½ cup coconut milk
½ cup fresh apple cider
Salt and freshly ground pepper
Chopped scallions
Chopped cilantro

Warm the oil in a deep, heavy soup pot set over medium-high heat, and cook the onion and celery until very soft, about 3 to 4 minutes. Stir in the curry powder, and cook for 30 seconds to 1 minute. Pour in the stock, and bring it to a boil. Reduce the heat to a simmer, and add the squash. Cook until the squash is tender, about 15 to 20 minutes.

Whisk in the coconut milk and cider, and season with salt and pepper. Serve the soup garnished with chopped scallions and cilantro.

Baby-blue hubbard squash is an heirloom variety with fairly dry, nutty-tasting, golden flesh.

Red Kuri Squash Stuffed with Wild Rice and Chickpea Pilaf

Serves 4

Red kuri, a beautiful, bright orange-red squash, is dense and honey sweet. This makes a very hearty side dish or a lovely vegetarian or vegan meal. Feel free to substitute another squash, such as butternut, acorn, or kabocha.

2 small red kuri squash
Sunflower oil
1 onion, chopped
8 ounces cremini mushrooms, trimmed and chopped
Salt and freshly ground pepper
½ cup vegetable stock (page 264)
½ cup dry white wine
2 cups cooked wild rice (page 229)
⅓ cup dried cranberries
¼ cup chopped parsley
1 tablespoon thyme leaves
1 teaspoon chopped sage
1 cup cooked chickpeas
½ cup chopped, toasted hazelnuts (page 265)

Preheat the oven to 400 degrees.

Cut the squash in half crosswise, and remove the seeds. Rub the cut sides with a little oil, and place the squash cut-side down on a baking sheet. Roast the squash until it is tender, about 25 minutes. Set the squash aside.

Film a large skillet with about 1 tablespoon of sunflower oil, and set it over medium-high heat. Sauté the onion and mushrooms until they are very soft and the onions begin to brown, about 7 to 10 minutes. Season the sauté with salt and pepper. Stir in the stock and wine, and simmer until the liquid is reduced by half. Stir in the wild rice, cranberries, parsley, thyme, sage, and chickpeas, and heat through. Taste and adjust the seasonings.

Turn the squash cut-side up, and spoon the wild rice mixture into the squash halves. Sprinkle the squash with the chopped hazelnuts. Return the squash to the oven and heat through.

Harvest Stuffed Squash

Serves 8

Use those darling little Cinderella pumpkins for this meatless alternative to Thanksgiving's turkey. The recipe is from Atina Diffley, cofounder of Gardens of Eagan (Farmington, Minnesota). At her table, it is a favorite that often doubles as a side dish and a meatless entree for vegetarians.

4 small Cinderella pumpkins or acorn squash, halved and seeded
2 tablespoons hazelnut oil or olive oil
1 large onion, chopped
4 cloves garlic, minced
1 fennel bulb, diced
1 red bell pepper, chopped
1 large carrot, finely diced
¼ cup chopped hazelnuts
2 cups cooked wild rice
½ cup chopped parsley
2 tablespoons rubbed sage
Salt and freshly ground pepper

Preheat the oven to 375 degrees. Place the squash cut-side down on a baking sheet and bake until it is tender, about 40 minutes.

Meanwhile, heat the oil in a large skillet set over medium-high heat, and sauté the onion, garlic, fennel, bell pepper, carrot, and hazelnuts until the onions are translucent, about 5 minutes. Add the wild rice, parsley, and sage, and season with salt and pepper to taste. Remove the squash from the oven, and turn it cut-side up on the baking sheet. Fill the squash with the stuffing. Return the squash to the oven, and bake it an additional 30 minutes.

Sunchokes

Jerusalem artichokes (aka sunchokes) are the roots of the sunflower plant. The name Jerusalem artichoke might have been a mispronunciation of the Italian word *girasol,* meaning "turning to the sun" (sunflowers). And they taste a little like globe artichokes. But they're not from Jerusalem, and they're not artichokes.

These knobby tubers are delicious raw. They're crisp and crunchy, with a texture and flavor reminiscent of water chestnuts. Cooked, they are moist, slightly sweet, and starchy—quite like chestnuts. They're delicious steamed or boiled and mashed in with potatoes; roasted; or sliced and tossed into stir-fries, sautés, soups, and stews. Just be warned: they are known to cause gas in some folks.

COOK'S NOTE

You can peel sunchokes, but they're often fine simply scrubbed. Sunchokes oxidize quickly after they're cut, so dip them in water with lemon juice before using them raw.
1 pound = 2 cups sliced sunchokes

Quick Ideas

Sautéed Sunchokes: Melt a tablespoon or so of butter in a skillet set over medium-high heat, and add a layer of thinly sliced sunchokes. Sauté until browned on both sides, about 7 to 10 minutes. Serve with a squeeze of lemon juice.

Mashed Sunchokes: Chop scrubbed sunchokes. Boil and mash them with the potatoes when making mashed potatoes.

Sunchokes and Baby Lettuces with Tarragon Vinaigrette

Serves 6

The crisp texture and nutty flavor of sunchokes shines in this tangy salad.

Juice of 1 small lemon
1 large shallot, minced
1 tablespoon Dijon mustard
¼ cup extra-virgin olive oil
1 teaspoon minced tarragon
Salt and freshly ground pepper
4 large sunchokes, scrubbed
6 ounces mixed spring lettuces (butter lettuce, baby spinach, etc.)
3 hard-boiled eggs, peeled and quartered

In a small bowl, whisk together 1 tablespoon of the lemon juice, the shallot, and the mustard. Whisk in the olive oil, the tarragon, and the salt and pepper.

Put the remaining lemon juice in a medium bowl. Slice the sunchokes into ½-inch rounds; then add them to the bowl and toss so that they are coated with the lemon juice.

Put the greens in a large bowl, and toss them with the vinaigrette. Drain the sunchokes, add them to the salad, and toss again. Serve garnished with the eggs.

Angel Hair Pasta and Sunchokes in Lemon Cream

Serves 2 to 4

Cooked sunchokes have a velvety texture and a nutty flavor that is nicely matched to the gin, with its hints of juniper, in this spirited pasta.

2 lemons
3 medium sunchokes, scrubbed
1 cup heavy cream
½ cup gin
12 ounces angel hair pasta
Salt and freshly ground pepper
¼ cup chopped parsley
2 tablespoons chopped basil

Set a large pot of salted water over high heat and bring it to a boil.

Finely grate the zest of one lemon, and set the zest aside. Juice both lemons into a medium dish. Cut the sunchokes into ½-inch slices and add them to the lemon juice, turning to coat.

In a large skillet over medium heat, combine the cream and the gin. Drain the lemon juice from the sunchokes, and stir them into the cream. Lower the heat, and simmer until the cream thickens slightly and the sunchokes soften, about 5 minutes.

Cook the pasta until it is just al dente, drain it, and toss it into the skillet along with the lemon zest. Heat gently, tossing the pasta with the sauce. Season with salt and freshly ground pepper. Stir in the parsley and basil and serve.

Garnet sweet potatoes are a little moister than other varieties and are mildly sweet. They should be this size at harvest; any bigger and they do not keep well.

Sweet Potatoes

Sweet potatoes are not yams. Yams originated in Africa and do not grow here. The varieties of sweet potatoes you'll find in our markets are smaller, ruddier, drier, and in most cases, sweeter than those that grow in southern climes. Sweet potatoes are tricky to grow, but our farmers have figured out how to control their environment and trap the sun's heat using hoop houses and high towers to produce vibrant crops. Sweet potatoes are super vegetables, loaded with antioxidants, vitamins A and K, and more than twice the amount of vitamin C of white potatoes.

COOK'S NOTE

Savory or sweet, sweet potatoes are delicious. Use the puréed flesh in muffins and cakes or to thicken savory stews and soups. Be careful to bake whole sweet potatoes in a baking dish or on a roasting pan to catch their syrupy juices as they bake.

1 pound = 1 large or 2 small sweet potatoes = 2 to 3 cups diced

Quick Ideas

Roasted Sweet Potatoes: Place the sweet potatoes on a roasting pan, and roast them in a 350-degree oven until very tender, about 45 to 60 minutes, depending on size. Slit open the skins, and season with soy sauce or balsamic vinegar.

Whipped Sweet Potatoes: Roast sweet potatoes as directed above. Slit the skins and scoop out the sweet flesh. Put it in a pot, and whip in a little melted butter, cinnamon, nutmeg, salt, and pepper to taste. Serve hot.

Stuffed Roasted Sweet Potatoes: Roast several sweet potatoes as directed above. Slice off the top third of the sweet potato, and scoop out some of the flesh. Fill the hollow with salsa and shredded cheese, a drizzle of honey and chopped nuts, or curry powder and toasted coconut.

Sweet Potato Fries

Serves 4

Make more of these than you think you will need because at least half will be picked from the sheet before they even get to the serving plate.

2 medium sweet potatoes, peeled
2 tablespoons sunflower oil
1 tablespoon maple syrup
Coarse salt and freshly ground pepper

Preheat oven to 450 degrees. Cut the sweet potatoes in half lengthwise, and cut each half into long spears. Place them on a baking sheet, and toss them with the oil. Spread the potatoes in one layer. Combine the maple syrup, salt, and pepper, and drizzle it over the potatoes. Bake for 15 minutes, turn the sweet potatoes, and then bake for another 5 to 10 minutes, until slightly browned.

Gingered Sweet Potatoes with Orange and Cranberries

Serves 4 to 6

This bright matchup of ruby cranberries, tart orange juice, and mellow sweet potatoes makes a brilliant holiday side dish.

2 tablespoons sunflower oil
1 onion, minced
2 tablespoons grated ginger
2 pounds sweet potatoes, peeled and cut into thin strips
¼ cup fresh cranberries
¼ cup fresh orange juice

Heat the oil in a large sauté pan over medium heat, sauté the onion until it is translucent, about 3 to 5 minutes, and then stir in the ginger. Toss in the sweet potatoes, cranberries, and orange juice. Cover the pan, reduce the heat to simmer, and cook until the sweet potatoes are tender but not falling apart, about 5 to 10 minutes.

Sweet Potato Soup with Ginger and Warm Spices

Serves 4 to 6

Warming and spicy, this lush soup is creamy but contains no cream. Serve it garnished with chopped fresh mint and cilantro.

1 tablespoon sunflower oil or vegetable oil
1 medium yellow onion, chopped
2 cloves garlic, minced
1 tablespoon grated ginger
½ teaspoon ground cardamom
2 pounds sweet potatoes, peeled and cut into chunks
5 to 6 cups vegetable stock or chicken stock (page 264)
½ cup coconut milk
½ cup fresh orange juice, or more to taste
2 teaspoons orange zest
1 tablespoon honey, or more to taste
Salt and freshly ground pepper
Pinch of crushed red pepper
¼ cup chopped fresh mint
¼ cup chopped fresh cilantro

In a soup pot over low heat, heat the oil and sauté the onions until they're very soft, about 10 minutes. Add the garlic, and cook another minute.

Increase the heat and add the ginger, cardamom, sweet potatoes, and enough stock to cover. Bring to a boil, reduce the heat to medium-low, and simmer, partially covered, until the potatoes are very soft, about 15 minutes.

Purée the soup in batches and return it to the pot, or use an immersion blender. Stir in the coconut milk, orange juice, zest, honey, and, if the soup is too thick, a little more stock or water. Season to taste with salt, pepper, and crushed red pepper. Serve garnished with mint and cilantro.

Tomatillos

Tomatillos are not tomatoes; instead, they're related to the Cape gooseberry. Covered in a thin, light-green papery skin, the fruit is firm and green and prized for its sharp, clean taste. Tomatillos and cilantro have such an affinity for each other that it's hard to think of one without imagining the other.

COOK'S NOTE
To use tomatillos, simply remove their papery skins.
1 pound = 12 tomatillos = about 2 cups diced

Quick Ideas

Tomatillo Salsa: Coarsely chop a pound of tomatillos. Put them in a blender or a food processor fitted with a steel blade, and purée with 2 seeded and sliced jalapeños, 1 cup of cilantro leaves, 2 cloves of garlic, 1 tablespoon of lime juice, and salt and pepper to taste.

Roasted Tomatillos: Set out roasted tomatillos as a condiment for tacos, burritos, or burgers. Simply peel the tomatillos, and roast them on a grill over high heat, turning so that all the surfaces are charred, about 5 minutes. Remove and slice.

Mexican Chicken Stew

Serves 6

Make this stew well ahead of time so the flavors mellow and mingle. Serve it with hunks of cornbread or over rice.

¼ cup flour
½ teaspoon salt
1 teaspoon ground pepper
½ teaspoon ground cumin
3 pounds boneless, skinless chicken thighs, cut into 3-inch pieces
2 tablespoons sunflower oil
1 onion, chopped
2 cloves garlic, chopped
2 cups chopped tomatillos
1 small jalapeño, seeded and chopped
1 tablespoon marjoram leaves
½ cup chopped cilantro
1 cup chicken stock or vegetable stock (page 264)
Sour cream or strained plain yogurt

In a medium bowl, stir together the flour, salt, pepper, and cumin. Add the chicken, and toss until it is coated in the flour mixture.

Heat the oil in a large heavy pan or Dutch oven over medium-high heat. Working in batches, sear the chicken until it is browned on all sides, about 10 minutes. Remove, and set aside.

Add the onion to the pan, and cook until it is translucent. Stir in the garlic, tomatillos, jalapeño, marjoram, cilantro, and stock. Scrape any browned bits that cling to the bottom of the pan. Return the chicken to the pan, and adjust the seasoning. Reduce the heat, and simmer, covered and stirring occasionally, until the chicken is very tender, about 30 to 45 minutes. Serve garnished with sour cream.

Fiery Green Sauce

Makes 1 ½ cups

Serve this hot and tangy sauce instead of ketchup on burgers, hot dogs, and fries. It also perks up scrambled eggs, nachos, burritos, and chips.

8 large tomatillos, peeled
1 large jalapeño
1 onion, chopped
3 cloves garlic, chopped
1 tablespoon oregano
½ cup vegetable stock (page 264)
½ cup chopped cilantro
Juice of half a lime
Salt and freshly ground pepper

Roast the tomatillos and the jalapeño on a grill or under a broiler, turning them so all of the surfaces become charred and blistered. Remove, and cover them with a towel to loosen the skins.

Peel the tomatillos, and peel and seed the jalapeño.

Put the tomatillos, jalapeño, onion, garlic, oregano, and stock into a blender and purée. Pour the mixture into a saucepan, and bring it to a boil. Reduce the heat, and simmer until the sauce thickens, about 8 minutes. Remove the sauce from the heat, add the cilantro and lime, and season with salt and pepper to taste. Use the sauce hot or cold.

Cilantro is a must in salsa. Whenever a recipe calls for tomatillos, add some cilantro too.

Tomatoes

Come August, our markets brim with tomatoes. Big fat Brandywines, sugary Sun Gold cherries, striped zebras, light yellow Taxis, shockingly orange Jaune Flamme—the list of exotic, heirloom, and foreign varieties grows by the year. Thank goodness. If our growers were not devoting time and energy to cultivating so many different types, we'd be stuck eating those cottony commercial tomatoes notable only for their shipping and storage attributes. In summer, I want real tomatoes. Now.

Some tomatoes are best eaten fresh, while others are suited to cooking in sauces and soups. They are, for the most part, interchangeable, but it's best to taste the different varieties to get a sense of what works with what.

COOK'S NOTE

To seed and peel? According to several tomato connoisseurs, most of the tomato's flavor is in the gel that surrounds the seeds. Remove the seeds, the gel comes too, and you've lessened the taste. As far as peels go, some think that the rough bits add rustic texture and leave them in; others, of course, disagree.

The easiest solution is to run the tomatoes through a food mill that will press and sort the gel from the seeds and catch the odd bits of skin as the tomato moves through.

Roma tomatoes are best for cooking into soup and sauce.

1 pound = 4 cups chopped tomatoes

Quick Ideas

Fresh Tomato Sauce:
Quickly chop together a pint of cherry tomatoes, ½ cup of fresh basil leaves, and 1 clove of garlic. Toss with just a little olive oil and a sprinkle of balsamic vinegar. Serve with bruschetta or big crackers. Or toss the sauce with freshly drained hot pasta.

Blackened Tomatoes:
Blackening gives tomatoes a smoky taste and makes them very easy to peel. (Use blackened tomatoes in the Fresh Tomato Sauce recipe for a bolder taste.) Place the tomatoes on a wire rack directly over a gas burner or on a medium-high grill. Turn them frequently until they're blackened over their entire surface. Remove the tomatoes from the grill, and slide off their skins.

Roasted Tomatoes:
Roasting condenses the already intense flavor of cherry tomatoes. They shrivel and sweeten and are terrific on top of bruschetta, alongside roast chicken, on top of pizza. Toss a pint of cherry tomatoes with enough olive oil to coat. Spread them on a baking sheet, and roast them at 400 degrees until they darken and shrivel, about 20 to 35 minutes, depending on their size.

Opposite: Oh, tomatoes! There's no end to the vast variety of heirloom tomatoes – yellow Taxi, golden pear, Russian black, Jersey boy, Zebra – all succulent when ripe and all slightly different in flavor.

Tomato Potato Gratin

Serves 6 to 8

Late summer meets early fall in this dish. Make it when the baby potatoes are just coming in and the tomato crop has just passed its peak. Vary the cheeses: feta and cheddar work nicely here. While most often served as a side dish, this also works nicely for a main course.

3 tablespoons extra-virgin olive oil
1 medium onion, thinly sliced
Salt and freshly ground pepper
2 pounds baby red, Yukon Gold, or Yellow Finn potatoes, thinly sliced
¼ cup chopped basil
1 tablespoon chopped parsley
2 pounds tomatoes of mixed colors and sizes, thinly sliced
¼ cup white wine
¼ cup shredded Parmesan

Preheat the oven to 375 degrees.

Use just a little of the oil to grease a 9-inch gratin dish. Distribute the onion slices over the bottom of the dish, and season them with salt and pepper. Arrange a layer of potato slices over the onions, followed by a little salt and pepper, a sprinkling of basil and parsley, and then a layer of tomatoes. Continue alternating layers of potatoes, seasoning and herbs, and tomatoes. Pour in the wine.

Cover the dish tightly with aluminum foil, and bake until the potatoes have softened, about 45 to 50 minutes. Uncover the dish, sprinkle the cheese over top, return it to the oven, and continue baking until the cheese is nicely browned. Serve warm or at room temperature.

Tomato Jam

Makes 1 quart, 2 pints, or 4 half-pints

Spicy and sweet tomato jam is terrific on grilled chicken, sandwiches, and bruschetta. Swirl it into mayonnaise or sour cream for a dip.

4 green cardamom pods
1 tablespoon coriander seeds
1 tablespoon cumin seeds
3 whole cloves
1 teaspoon peppercorns
4 pounds tomatoes (mixed varieties), chopped
Juice and zest of 1 small orange
Juice and zest of 1 lime
1 cup sugar
Salt and freshly ground pepper

Prepare a stockpot or canner and jars (see page 51).

Use a spice mill or a mortar and pestle to grind the spices together. Put the tomatoes in a large heavy pan with the spices, grated zests, and orange and lime juices. Add the sugar, and then add salt and pepper to taste. Set the pan over medium heat, and stir until the sugar has dissolved. Reduce the heat and simmer, stirring regularly, until the mixture becomes thick, at least 30 minutes, and continue simmering until the mixture holds its shape and becomes the consistency of soft jam.

Ladle the hot liquid into the warm jars, leaving ½-inch of headspace. Wipe the jar rims, center the lids on the jars, and screw on the bands until they are just finger tight.

Place the jars in the canner, ensuring they are completely covered with water. Bring to a boil, and process for 15 minutes. Turn off the heat, remove the canner lid, and let the jars remain in the hot water for another 5 minutes. Remove the jars, let them cool, and then store them in a cool, dark place.

Straight-Up Salsa

Serves 8

Variations on salsa are endless, so feel free to toss in chopped apples, tomatillos, peppers, whatever you wish. Salsa shouldn't be too chunky or over-diced—think of how the salsa will sit on a chip. Plum tomatoes work beautifully, but any fresh bright tomato will do.

4 plum tomatoes, chopped
4 scallions, chopped
½ cup minced onion
¼ cup chopped cilantro
1 clove garlic, minced
1 small jalapeño, seeded, deveined, and minced
2 tablespoons fresh lime juice

Combine all of the ingredients in one bowl and season to taste with salt and pepper.

Simply Tomato Sauce

Makes 4 cups

This is a go-to sauce. It is great tossed with pasta, spread on pizza, spooned over sautéed chicken. Make an extra batch to can or freeze for later. You'll enjoy it when the winter wind howls outside your door.

1 tablespoon olive oil or vegetable oil
5 cloves garlic, minced
6 cups chopped plum tomatoes
½ cup chopped basil
1 tablespoon oregano
Salt and freshly ground pepper

Put the oil in a large pot, and set it over medium heat. When the oil shimmers, add the garlic and sauté, stirring constantly, for about 15 to 30 seconds, watching that the garlic doesn't burn. Add the tomatoes, basil, and oregano and bring the sauce to a boil. Reduce the heat to low and simmer the sauce about 20 to 25 minutes. For a smooth sauce, run it through a food mill or strainer. For a rustic sauce, leave it as is. Season to taste with salt and pepper.

Panzanella

Serves 4 to 8

I never tire of this classic tomato bread salad; it's a great showcase for ripe tomatoes, bursting and ready to eat. The variations are endless: you might crisp the bread in advance by sautéing it in a little olive oil or butter (as croutons) or toss in chopped peppers, cucumbers, and chunks of feta cheese. Use a variety of tomatoes. Because there's no mayonnaise in this dressing, the salad travels beautifully and holds nicely for a picnic or backyard barbecue.

2 pounds tomatoes (mixed varieties), cored and coarsely chopped
1 Anaheim chili, deveined and thinly sliced (optional)
2 thick slices coarse white bread such as ciabatta
3 cloves garlic, crushed
3 tablespoons extra-virgin olive oil
2 tablespoons red wine vinegar, balsamic vinegar, or sherry vinegar
1 small red onion, thinly sliced
½ cup pitted and sliced kalamata olives
2 tablespoons capers, drained
1 generous cup sliced basil
½ cup sliced parsley
Salt and freshly ground pepper

Put the tomatoes in a large bowl with the chili. Tear the bread into small chunks and add it to the bowl. Toss in the garlic, oil, vinegar, onion, olives, and capers and stir to combine. Add the basil, parsley, salt, and pepper. Allow the salad to sit for at least 15 minutes or up to 4 hours before serving.

Chilled Tomato Soup

Serves 4 to 6

This speedy version of gazpacho is colorful and refreshing, especially on a sweltering August night. Top it off with a jigger of vodka, and it doubles as a cocktail.

3 shallots, diced
Balsamic vinegar, sherry vinegar, or red wine vinegar
4 to 5 pounds ripe red tomatoes of various sizes, including cherry tomatoes
2 tablespoons salt
1 cucumber, peeled, seeded, and diced
Salt and freshly ground pepper
Chopped basil

Put the shallots in a small bowl, cover them with the vinegar, and set aside. Quarter the tomatoes, turn them into a large bowl, toss them with the salt, and set them aside for about 30 minutes.

Work the tomatoes through a food mill to make a thick sauce, or purée them in a blender and then strain the sauce if you wish to remove the seeds and skins. Scoop out the shallots (reserving the vinegar) and add them, along with the cucumber, to the tomato sauce. Season to taste with the vinegar, salt, and pepper. Refrigerate. Serve well chilled, garnished with chopped basil.

Turnips
2.00/bunch

Turnips

Turnips are mild and tender in the spring. As they mature, they become more robust. Once the ground freezes, they turn surprisingly sweet. Turnips store beautifully and so are at market through the winter. The freshest young spring turnips taste like radishes and are great eaten raw. The white Japanese Tokyo turnip is most familiar, but the farmers at market are growing surprising varieties such as purple-shouldered French turnips, red turnips with burnished skin and pearly white flesh, yellow turnips (a pale sunny color inside and out), and long, tapered turnips with rosy tops.

COOK'S NOTE

Turnips and rutabagas are not the same, though they're often confused (yellow turnips resemble small rutabagas). Turnip greens, especially the tops of baby turnips, are delicious sautéed.
1 pound = 2 cups chopped turnips

Quick Ideas

Sautéed Turnips and Greens: This dish calls for just-picked baby turnips. Cut a handful of baby turnips from their greens. Scrub the turnips; then trim and slice thin. Remove the ribs and stems from the greens, and set the greens aside. Film a skillet with oil, and set it over medium-high heat. Add the sliced turnips and sauté, stirring occasionally, until slightly browned, about 5 minutes. Toss in the greens, cover the pan, and cook until the greens are nicely wilted. Toss with a little red wine vinegar or balsamic vinegar before serving.

Pan-Fried Turnips with Maple Glaze: Melt a tablespoon or two of butter in a large skillet over medium-low heat. Sauté 1 pound of diced turnips, cover the pan, and cook until the turnips are tender, about 5 minutes. Add a couple of tablespoons of maple syrup, and toss to coat. Serve with a sprinkle of salt and pepper and chopped parsley.

Spring Root Veggie Ragout

Serves 4

Baby turnips and carrots shine in this simple, delicate ragout. It comes together quickly.

1 tablespoon unsalted butter
8 spring onions, halved
8 small turnips, scrubbed and cut into ½-inch slices
5 small radishes, scrubbed and cut into ½-inch slices
5 carrots, scrubbed and cut into ½-inch pieces
2 sprigs thyme
¼ cup vegetable stock (page 264) or white wine
2 cups baby spinach
1 to 2 tablespoons fresh lemon juice
Salt and freshly ground pepper
¼ cup chopped basil

In a large skillet, melt the butter over medium-high heat. Sauté the onions, turnips, radishes, and carrots with the thyme sprigs for 3 minutes. Add the stock, cover, and reduce the heat. Cook until the vegetables are tender, about 10 minutes. Toss in the spinach, and cook just until wilted. Season with lemon juice and salt and pepper. Toss in the basil, and serve right away.

Turnips with Bacon and Orange

Serves 4 to 6

The assertive, peppery bite of turnips cuts through bacon's salt and heft in this dish, which is sparked with a little orange. Boldly flavored, rich but not heavy, this is a terrific wintery dish.

3 strips smoked bacon, diced
1 onion, diced
½ cup white wine
Juice of 1 large orange
4 medium turnips, diced

In a medium skillet set over medium heat, cook the bacon until crisp, about 5 to 7 minutes. Remove, and set aside to drain on a paper towel. Discard all but 1 tablespoon of the rendered bacon fat, and return the pan to the heat. Add the onion, and sauté until it's just golden. Then add the wine, and deglaze the pan. Add the orange juice and the turnips and stir. Cover, lower the heat, and simmer until the turnips are tender, about 5 minutes. Remove the lid, and continue cooking until the liquid is nearly evaporated. Serve garnished with the bacon.

Watercress

Watercress is an exceptional green that serves as a salad green as well as an herb. It is one of the first greens to appear at market. Vibrant and spicy, it's just what I need to wake up my winter-weary palate. Watercress perks up any salad, is delicious tucked under a steak, and tastes wonderful mashed into pesto or swirled into mayonnaise.

COOK'S NOTE

Watercress becomes even hotter and spicier as spring turns to summer. Be sure to taste it before using the leaves.

1 pound = 4 to 6 cups of watercress leaves

Watercress and Blue Cheese Butter

Makes ½ cup

This peppery green grows along the icy banks of fast, clear streams in early spring. It's easy enough to find and pick in the woods. But it's even easier to get it at the market, freshly picked and cleaned. This rich spread is great on hamburgers and steak, or on bruschetta topped with roasted red pepper or sliced tomato.

3 ounces blue cheese
2 tablespoons unsalted butter, softened
½ cup loosely packed watercress sprigs, stemmed

In a food processor fitted with a steel blade, pulse together the blue cheese and the butter. Then pulse in the watercress. Scrape the butter into a dish or shape it into a log. Store in the refrigerator, covered.

Quick Ideas

Watercress Sandwiches: Generously spread unsalted butter over thin slices of white bread. Lay watercress leaves over the butter and sprinkle with a little coarse sea salt.

Watercress Dip: Chop ¼ cup of watercress, and stir it into ¼ cup of mayonnaise and ¼ cup of sour cream or strained plain yogurt. Serve the dip with crudités or chips.

Watercress, Melon, and Mint Salad

Serves 4

This makes a fine side salad and a wonderful condiment for grilled chicken or fish.

2 cups loosely packed watercress leaves, stemmed
1 cup loosely packed mint leaves
2 cups diced cantaloupe, honeydew, or both
¼ cup fresh lemon juice
2 tablespoons honey
Pinch of crushed red pepper
½ cup sunflower oil
Salt and freshly ground pepper

In a large bowl, toss together the watercress, mint leaves, and melon.

In a small bowl, whisk together the lemon juice, honey, and crushed red pepper, and then whisk in the oil. Toss the salad with the dressing, season with salt and pepper, and serve immediately.

Zucchini and Summer Squash

Zucchini and summer squash are too often the bane of the backyard. They grow like crazy and take over a plot, becoming baseball bats before our eyes. Better to get the tiny, firm squash from the farmers market (where you can find pretty, delicate squash flowers as well).

COOK'S NOTE

Green zucchini and yellow summer squash are similar in size and cooking qualities. Pattypan squash are round and flat with scalloped edges. Though these squashes have different sizes and shapes, they behave generally the same in recipes.

1 pound = 4 cups chopped squash or zucchini

Quick Ideas

Zucchini and Summer Squash with Garlic and Basil: Cut 1 pound of squash into thin slices. Film a large sauté pan with some oil, and set it over medium heat. Sauté the squash with several whole cloves of garlic until the squash is tender and just beginning to brown. Season the squash with salt, pepper, a squirt of lemon juice, and a big handful of chopped basil.

Zucchini Bread and Muffins: Toss shredded zucchini or summer squash into your favorite muffin recipe (about ½ cup per 12 muffins or 1 loaf of bread). Increase the baking time about 5 to 10 minutes to compensate for the moisture the zucchini adds.

Sautéed Squash Blossoms: Open the blossoms, and check for bugs. Place a small piece of fresh mozzarella and a little basil into each blossom, and twist it closed. Film a large skillet with olive oil, and sauté the blossoms, being careful not to crowd the pan, until they begin to brown, about 3 minutes. Serve right away.

Simplest Summer Soup with Garlic Toasts

Serves 6

This soup is a garden in a bowl. Vary the vegetables depending on what you have on hand. It's a terrific way to use up the odds and ends from your market bag or CSA box.

SOUP:

1 tablespoon sunflower oil or olive oil
1 medium onion, diced
1 carrot, diced
1 stalk celery, diced
2 sprigs thyme
1 small leek, white and green parts chopped
1 large tomato, diced (about 1 cup)
1 medium summer squash or zucchini, diced
1 Yukon Gold potato, peeled and diced
4 cups vegetable stock (page 264)
8 ounces green beans, cut into 1-inch pieces

GARLIC TOASTS:

6 baguette slices
Olive oil
Freshly ground pepper
2 tablespoons pesto (page 135)

Heat the oil in a large soup pot. Sauté the onion, carrot, celery, and thyme until the onion is transparent, about 5 to 7 minutes. Add the leek, tomato, squash, potato, and vegetable stock. Bring the stock to a boil; then reduce the heat and simmer the soup until the potatoes are soft but not falling apart, about 15 minutes. Add the green beans, and cook until they are tender, about 5 more minutes.

Preheat the broiler to high. Drizzle the baguette slices with olive oil, and grind some pepper over them. Broil until toasted, about 1 to 2 minutes. Spread equal amounts of pesto over each crouton. Ladle the soup into bowls, and float a crouton in each bowl of soup.

Braised Summer Squash and Zucchini with Herbs

Serves 4 to 6

This recipe is so simple and so good, as the zucchini and summer squash become meltingly tender and golden. Use the youngest zucchini and summer squash you can find.

2 tablespoons sunflower oil or olive oil
1 pound summer squash, sliced ¼-inch thick
1 pound zucchini, sliced ¼-inch thick
2 tablespoons fresh lemon juice
¼ cup chopped basil
¼ cup chopped parsley
Salt and freshly ground pepper
2 or 3 slices bread

Film a large skillet with the oil and set it over medium-high heat. Add the squash and zucchini and cook, stirring occasionally, until it becomes tender and begins to turn golden, about 20 minutes. Add the lemon juice and continue cooking a few more minutes. Toss in the basil and parsley, and season to taste with salt and pepper.

While the squash cooks, toast the bread. Put the toast in a food processor fitted with a steel blade and pulse until you have crumbs. Top the squash with ¼ cup of the bread crumbs just before serving.

Ratatouille

Serves 4 to 6

This summer classic uses the very best of our crops all in one dish—zucchini, eggplant, tomatoes, and lots and lots of garlic. Double the recipe; ratatouille is delicious served hot or at room temperature for lunch.

1 medium eggplant, sliced 1 inch thick
Extra-virgin olive oil or sunflower oil
1 onion, sliced 1 inch thick
5 cloves garlic, smashed
Pinch of crushed red pepper
1 large red bell pepper, seeded and sliced 1 inch thick
1 zucchini or summer squash, sliced 1 inch thick
2 pattypan squash, sliced 1 inch thick
3 medium tomatoes, cored and sliced 1 inch thick
½ cup chopped basil
Salt and freshly ground pepper

Toss the eggplant with some salt, and allow it to drain in a colander while you prepare the other vegetables.

Heat the oil in a heavy skillet set over medium-high heat. Sauté the onion until it is soft and translucent; then add the garlic and crushed red pepper. Toss in the bell pepper and cook for a few minutes; then add the squash and tomatoes. Cook, stirring occasionally, until the vegetables begin to wilt, about 5 minutes. Stir in the eggplant, cover, and cook until the eggplant is very soft and the flavors have melded together, about 30 minutes. Toss in the basil, and season to taste with salt and freshly ground pepper.

Summer squash, like these pattypans, may be used in stir-fries, salads, soups, and stews.

Cheese

Cheese

Why seek European imports when some of the world's best cheeses are right here? Local farmers are making award-winning cheese, yogurt, and skyr (an Icelandic dairy product similar to strained yogurt) on their farms with milk from their sheep, cows, and goats. Cheese made from the milk of grazing animals changes depending on the season. Spring's mild clover, summer's fragrant timothy, fall's late grasses, and winter's hay affect milk's flavor. Whether the cheese is brined, rubbed in herbs, or washed also helps determine its character, as does how long it is aged. Here is a general guide to our local farmers market cheeses (but new cheeses enter the market every week). The best way to learn about local cheeses is to talk to the farmers and taste their cheeses. Each cheese tastes of its locale as well as the craft of its maker.

SHEEP CHEESE

We live in a great region for raising sheep and thus for making cheese out of this rich, sweet milk. Sheep are hardy animals and, when cared for properly, can remain on pasture until well after the snow flies.

Generally speaking, the market's sheep cheeses range from full-flavored blue (modeled after French Roquefort) to semi-hard piquant Manchego-style to light, fresh cheeses that are creamier and sweeter than chèvre (goat cheese) but have more character than young cow's milk cheese.

GOAT CHEESE

Our local goat cheeses reflect a range of ethnic influences—French (creamy, tangy chèvre), Greek (salty, firm feta), and Latino (mild and springy queso fresco). Look for local chèvre marinated in olive oil with herbs and spices or sweetened with maple syrup and honey to lush effect.

COW CHEESE

Colby cheese was born in Wisconsin and remains the most popular choice in this region for its mild flavor and versatility. Look for hand-crafted cheddar, Gouda, Edam, and Swiss made in small batches. Most notable, Bent River (a Camembert-style cheese from Alemar Cheese Company), a relative newcomer, is made with local single-source milk.

CAVE-AGED CHEESE

At LoveTree, the specially designed aging cave siphons in a "tule" fog that contributes the flavors of the North Woods to Mary Falk's artisanal sheep milk cheeses. And Shepherd's Way Farms has specially designed an aging room to replicate the perfect cave environment for its Roquefort-style cheese.

These cheeses have distinct flavors, and they are pricey. Serve them simply—with crackers, fruit, and nuts—and keep these things in mind:

- Avoid sourdough bread (it's too tangy and interferes with the cheeses' flavors, especially delicate cheeses).
- Use unseasoned baguettes and crackers, with perhaps a few olives or nuts, for an appetizer.
- For dessert, serve the cheese with a baguette or crackers and a pot of local honey on the side.

To store cheeses:

- Wrap hard cheeses in butcher, waxed, or parchment paper, and store in the refrigerator's vegetable or meat and cheese compartment.
- Wrap and store soft, fresh cheeses as you would hard cheeses, but keep checking to be sure they are neither drying out nor getting funky. Use up soft cheeses right away.

LoveTree's cave-aged sheep's-milk cheese has won numerous national and international awards.

Chèvre Cheese Spread

Makes about 1 ¼ cups

Serve this with thinly sliced walnut bread or crackers. Leftovers are great as a sandwich spread. The spread will keep at least a week in the refrigerator.

8 ounces chèvre
2 to 3 tablespoons heavy cream or yogurt
2 to 3 tablespoons extra-virgin olive oil
2 tablespoons chopped herbs (parsley, chives, tarragon, dill—alone or
    in combination), plus a little more for garnish
1 tablespoon finely grated lemon zest
Coarse salt and freshly ground pepper

Using a food processor with a metal blade or a wooden spoon and a medium bowl, cream together the cheese, cream, and olive oil to make a thick spread; add more cream if needed. Work in the herbs and lemon zest, and season with salt and pepper.

Line a small bowl with a sheet of parchment paper or plastic wrap, and fill it with the cheese mixture. Cover, and chill for at least 30 minutes or overnight.

To serve, invert the bowl onto a serving platter and peel off the plastic. With the back of a spoon, level off the top of the cheese and make a small depression. Drizzle a bit of olive oil over the top. Sprinkle with a few more chopped herbs for garnish.

Apple, Walnut, and Blue Cheese Salad

Serves 4 to 6

Choose a big, robust blue or any strong, aged cheese for this salad.

WALNUT OIL VINAIGRETTE:

3 tablespoons white wine vinegar or apple cider vinegar

1 small shallot, minced

1 teaspoon Dijon mustard

½ cup walnut oil

Salt and freshly ground pepper

SALAD:

About 4 to 6 cups torn greens, trimmed, washed, and dried

1 tart apple, cored and cut into 1-inch pieces

¼ cup crumbled Big Woods Blue cheese

¼ cup chopped toasted walnuts (see page 265)

To make the vinaigrette, put the vinegar, shallot, mustard, and walnut oil in a jar, cover, and shake vigorously. Season the vinaigrette to taste with salt and pepper. You need about ¼ cup of the dressing for this salad; leftovers will store about a week in the refrigerator.

Toss the greens with just enough vinaigrette to lightly coat the leaves, and then arrange them on a large platter or individual plates. Toss the apple and cheese with a bit more of the vinaigrette, and pile them on top of the greens. Sprinkle the walnuts on top.

Grains

Whole Grains

We live in the nation's breadbasket; our region was built on the growing and milling of grain. Thank goodness our farmers are rediscovering heirloom varieties of grain. Besides providing much-needed crop diversity, these grains are highly nutritious and delicious. Currently, 80 percent of the nation's agricultural production is devoted to raising grains for animals. But, if we are to have a vibrant local food system (and landscape), then it's the ancient and vigorous grain crops that offer us hope for the future. When grown organically, farro (aka emmer), spelt, einkorn, and other ancient strains of wheat, plus rye, millet, barley, and oats, are wonderful eaten whole or milled into flour.

Here's a guide to what you might find.

Barley: Local barley is nutty tasting and highly nutritious, especially when sold hulled but not pearled. Pearl barley has been polished to remove the bran, sacrificing nutrients to speed the cooking time. To cook barley, use 1 part grain to 3 parts water. Simmer over medium heat until the grains have split, about 60 to 70 minutes.

Farro (also called emmer wheat): Farro looks like large brown barley and is beloved throughout Italy. It cooks quickly and is great in soups, stews, and grain salads. To cook farro, use 1 part grain to 3 parts water. Simmer over medium heat until the grains have split, about 20 to 30 minutes.

Spelt: This blond grain can be tough; it is best to presoak it before cooking. It's great in soups and stews. To cook spelt, use 1 part grain to 3 parts water. Simmer over medium heat until the grains have split, about 70 to 80 minutes.

Wheat berries (soft and hard): Hard red spring and hard winter wheat berries are high in protein and brownish in color. Soft wheat berries are lower in gluten content and paler in color. The differences between wheat berries are most noticeable when the grain is ground into flour. To cook wheat berries, use 1 part grain to 3 parts water. Simmer over medium heat until the grains have split, about 70 to 80 minutes.

Tuscan Farro Salad

Serves 4 to 6

This salad keeps nicely, travels well, and is perfect for picnics and barbecues. Serve it as a hearty side dish or a simple vegetarian entree. Vary the vegetables to suit the season. You can use just about any whole grain in this salad: cooked barley and wheat berries also work beautifully.

1 ½ cups farro
½ pound green beans cut into 1- to 2-inch pieces
½ cup pitted kalamata olives, sliced
1 red bell pepper, seeded and cut into thin strips
½ cup crumbled sharp cheese such as Parmesan or Asiago
¼ cup chopped chives
¼ cup chopped parsley
¼ cup chopped basil
¼ cup red wine vinegar
¼ cup olive oil or sunflower oil
1 tablespoon Dijon mustard
Salt and freshly ground pepper

In a medium saucepan, cover the farro with 2 inches of water and set the pan over high heat. Bring the water to a boil; then cover the pan, lower the heat, and simmer until the farro is tender, about 20 to 25 minutes. Drain; then transfer the grain to a large bowl and allow it to cool.

Bring another pot of water to a boil, and add the beans. Cook the beans until they are bright green, about 2 minutes. Drain, and refresh under cold water.

Combine the green beans, olives, bell pepper, cheese, chives, parsley, and basil with the farro.

In a small bowl, whisk together the vinegar, oil, and mustard. Toss the farro with the dressing, and season the salad with salt and pepper.

Harvest Grain and Bean Pilaf

Serves 4 to 6

Just about any grain will work in this pilaf, which makes a nutritious backdrop for local dried beans and fresh vegetables. It will hold nicely in the refrigerator, so feel free to make it ahead.

2 tablespoons sunflower oil
1 medium onion, diced
3 cloves garlic, smashed
½ cup diced celeriac
1 carrot, diced
1 tablespoon chopped oregano
½ cup dry white wine
½ cup chicken stock or vegetable stock (page 264)
1 cup diced tomato
2 cups cooked shell beans (page 68)
2 cups cooked barley, farro, or spelt (pages 226–27)
¼ cup chopped parsley
Pinch of crushed red pepper
Salt and freshly ground pepper
¼ cup grated Parmesan

Heat the oil in a large skillet set over medium-high heat, and cook the onion, garlic, celeriac, and carrot until the onion is translucent, about 5 minutes. Add the oregano, wine, stock, and tomatoes, and cook until the tomato is tender, about 3 minutes. Toss the cooked beans and grain into the vegetables along with the parsley. Season to taste with the crushed red pepper, salt, and freshly ground pepper. Serve warm topped with grated Parmesan.

Wild Rice

Find real, hand-harvested wild rice at the farmers markets from late summer through winter. It cooks quickly, and the flavor is nutty, woodsy, and beguiling. This rice grows wild in the clear northern lakes and is harvested by canoe: as one person poles the boat through the rice fields, the other knocks the grass seed into the boat with a pair of sticks called rice knockers. The grain is then dried, toasted over an open fire, and threshed in big baskets. This rice costs about three times as much as the cultivated rice, but once you taste it, you will understand why.

Basic Wild Rice

Serves 6 to 8

This recipe calls for hand-harvested wild rice, which is available in most grocery stores and natural food co-ops and at farmers markets. It's so tasty that you don't really need more than a pat of butter and a few chopped herbs. Leftovers freeze nicely.

1 cup wild rice, rinsed under cold water
2 ½ cups water or stock

In a large saucepan, combine the rice and the water. Set the pan over high heat, and bring the water to a boil. Reduce the heat, and simmer the rice until it is tender but not mushy, about 20 to 30 minutes.

Wild Rice Cranberry Pilaf

Serves 4 to 6

This is a natural partner to chicken, game, and pork. It makes a terrific dish for the holiday buffet table.

½ cup wild rice, rinsed under cold water
1 ¼ cups chicken stock (page 264) or water
1 tablespoon unsalted butter
1 shallot, finely chopped
1 small onion, finely chopped
2 tablespoons chopped parsley
1 (2-inch) sprig rosemary
¼ cup dried cranberries
1 teaspoon grated orange zest
⅓ cup fresh orange juice, or to taste
Salt and freshly ground pepper
¼ cup chopped toasted walnuts (see note)

In a large saucepan, combine the rice with the chicken stock. Bring the stock to a boil; then reduce the heat and simmer, uncovered, for 20 to 30 minutes. The rice should be tender but not mushy.

While the rice is cooking, melt the butter in a medium skillet over medium heat. Sauté the shallot, onion, parsley, and rosemary until the onion is translucent, about 2 to 4 minutes. Stir in the dried cranberries, orange zest, and orange juice, and cook about 2 minutes. Remove the rosemary sprig. Stir the sauté into the rice and season it with salt and pepper to taste. Fold in the walnuts. Serve hot or at room temperature.

Note: To toast the walnuts, spread the nuts on a baking sheet and toast in a preheated 350-degree oven until they begin to smell nutty, about 3 to 5 minutes. Remove and chop.

Wild Rice and Mushroom Soup

Serves 6 to 8

If you are lucky enough to have leftover wild rice, make this soup. The splash of cream called for here gives a lush, rich texture, but feel free to leave it out.

2 tablespoons unsalted butter
1 large onion, finely chopped
2 shallots, finely chopped
1 pound cremini or white button mushrooms, caps and stems roughly chopped
1 tablespoon all-purpose flour
Generous pinch of freshly grated nutmeg
¼ cup amber beer or red wine
3 cups chicken stock (page 264)
3 cups milk
¼ cup heavy cream
1 cup cooked wild rice (page 229)
Salt and freshly ground pepper
¼ cup chopped parsley

In a heavy-bottomed pot set over medium heat, melt the butter and sauté the onion, shallots, and mushrooms. Cover the pan, and cook until the onions are very soft and the mushrooms have released most of their liquid, about 7 to 10 minutes.

Reduce the heat to low. Sprinkle the vegetables with the flour and nutmeg, stir, and cook until the flour mixture coats the vegetables like a thick paste, about 1 minute. Whisk in the beer, stock, milk, and cream, and then stir in the wild rice. Simmer several minutes until the soup thickens to the desired consistency. Season with salt and pepper. Serve garnished with the parsley.

Fresh Flour

WHEAT FLOUR

Just one taste of freshly milled flour and you will understand why it makes a difference in baked goods. When milled just after harvest, the wheat kernels retain a little of the natural oils that give this flour its nutty fragrance and distinctive taste. Much of the fresh flour in our farmers markets comes from older strains of wheat that have a high gluten content, perfect for making breads and pizzas. Many of the farmers also sell their wheat berries to mill into flour at home.

Be sure to store freshly milled wheat in the refrigerator or freeze it. It is truly fresh, and left out in the air, its flavor disperses as the oils dry off.

CORNMEAL AND POLENTA

Mandan Bride is the princess of flour corn, and many of our farmers are growing this heritage crop to mill. It's a beautiful red and gold cob that, when ground, becomes a wonderful meal for bread or polenta. Because this corn is milled with its hulls (not hulled as commercial polenta corn is), it's loaded with nutrients and real corn flavor. Freshly ground cornmeal and polenta should be stored in the refrigerator or frozen.

Honey, Oat, Flax, and Sunny Quick Bread

Makes 1 loaf

This fragrant, tender bread is ready in no time. It's great served with cheese and soup or spread with jam for a treat. Here's where using fresh wheat flour makes a real difference.

1 ¼ cups all-purpose flour
1 cup whole wheat flour
2 teaspoons baking powder
¼ teaspoon baking soda
1 teaspoon salt
1 cup plain yogurt
1 large egg
¼ cup sunflower oil
¼ cup mild honey
¾ cup milk
1 cup old-fashioned rolled oats
¼ cup flax seeds
¼ cup sunflower seeds

Preheat the oven to 375 degrees. Grease and flour a 9 × 5-inch loaf pan.

In a large bowl, stir together the flours, baking powder, baking soda, and salt.

In a medium bowl, beat together the yogurt, egg, oil, honey, and milk, and then stir in the oats and flax seeds. Stir the wet mixture into the flour mixture just until blended; do not overmix. Scrape the batter into the prepared pan. Sprinkle with the sunflower seeds.

Bake the loaf until it is well browned on top and a toothpick inserted in the center comes out clean, 40 to 50 minutes. Let the loaf stand in the pan on a wire rack for 15 minutes. Run a knife around the edges of the loaf to loosen it, and then turn it out onto a rack.

Polenta

Serves 4

When you use freshly milled corn for polenta, the sweet taste of corn shines. Serve this topped simply with good butter, a sprinkling of cheese, or both. It's great finished with sautéed mushrooms, fresh corn, or chopped tomatoes and herbs.

2 ½ cups water
1 tablespoon salt
1 cup polenta or coarse cornmeal

Put the water and the salt in a large pot set over medium heat, and bring it to a simmer. Gradually add the polenta in a slow, steady stream, whisking all the while to prevent lumps. Simmer until the polenta is thick and creamy, about 10 to 15 minutes. The polenta should be the consistency of sour cream. Pour the polenta into a large, warmed serving bowl, and serve it with your choice of toppings.

Skillet Flatbreads

Makes 6 flatbreads

These quick yeasted breads have a toasty interior and a moist center. Top them with grated cheese to serve with soups and stews, or scatter sliced meat and vegetables over them to make a quick pizza.

FLATBREAD:

1 cup warm water
1 tablespoon sunflower oil
1 (2 ¼ teaspoons) package dry yeast
1 teaspoon honey
1 ½ cups to 2 cups all-purpose flour
1 cup whole wheat flour
1 teaspoon salt

TOPPINGS:

Grated Parmesan
Roasted red peppers and feta
Arugula and chèure
Tomatoes, basil, and mozzarella

Whisk together the water, oil, yeast, and honey in a large bowl. Let it stand until the yeast is foamy, about 5 minutes. Stir in 1 ½ cups of the all-purpose flour, all of the whole wheat flour, and the salt. Add just enough of the remaining flour to make a smooth but slightly sticky dough. Turn the dough onto a lightly floured work surface, and knead until the dough is smooth but still soft, about 5 minutes, adding more flour as needed.

Put the dough into a lightly oiled bowl, turning the dough to coat it with oil. Cover the dough with a clean dishtowel, and set it in a warm place to rise until it has doubled, about 1 to 1 ½ hours.

Punch the dough down, and divide it into 6 equal balls. Dust each with flour. Place a large skillet over medium-high heat. Roll or stretch each ball into a circle about 6 to 7 inches in diameter. Cook one flatbread at a time, turning it once, until browned on both sides and cooked through, about 30 seconds to 1 minute per side. Adjust the heat as needed to prevent burning.

Top the flatbreads with any of the toppings, and pop them in the oven to keep warm. Or, stack the cooked flatbreads on top of each other on a plate, and cover them with a clean towel. Let them cool completely before wrapping and storing them.

Meat and Fish

Beef and Bison

Pastured and grass-fed animals raised outside on grass produce a leaner beef that tastes "the way beef used to taste," before cattle were fed corn. Some ranchers use a hybrid process that keeps the cattle in pasture as they mature and then finishes them on corn and grain before

they go to market. This finishing helps develop the marbling and flavor of corn-fed beef.

Aging improves the flavor and texture of beef, infusing it with a buttery character and deeper flavor. Most steaks have been wet aged, a process that seals the meat in a vacuum pack and refrigerates it for a spell. Purists will argue that dry-aging beef by storing it unwrapped in a controlled environment for several weeks concentrates its flavor. Dry-aged beef is far higher in price than wet-aged beef, but once you taste it, you will understand why.

Buffalo or bison, bison or buffalo, the names can be confusing, but cooking the meat is the same. The American buffalo is bison (buffalo is the animal whose milk the Italians turn into mozzarella but is originally from China).

Bison are lower in fat than cattle. Their coats, not their interior fat, keep them warm. And because they live on pasture, not corn, their meat is especially high in conjugated linoleic acid (CLA). CLA is prized for its anticancer properties and its ability to reduce joint inflammation and support cardiovascular function.

Cook bison low and slow. Roasts should be cooked in a 275-degree oven to a temperature no higher than 120 degrees. Ground bison and bison burgers are exceptionally lean; cook these to rare.

COOK'S NOTE

Because grass-fed beef and bison are very low in fat, they should be cooked to a lower temperature than conventionally raised beef—that is, to no more than 120 to 125 degrees.

Quick Ideas

Steak Salads: Turn the odds and ends left from grilled steaks or roasts into salads with cooked dried beans and vinaigrette.

Carnitas: Use scraps trimmed from meat and small portions from larger cuts in carnitas. Simply toss the meat with a little oil, season it with salt, pepper, and chili powder, and roast on high until the meat is crisped. Serve carnitas over rice with salsa or roll it in a tortilla.

Stir-Fried Bison with Spring Vegetables

Serves 4 to 6

Serve this over cooked barley, farro, or pasta. It's quick and easy.

¼ cup hoisin sauce
1 tablespoon soy sauce
1 tablespoon dark sesame oil
2 cloves garlic, smashed
1 pound bison sirloin steak
2 tablespoons sunflower oil or vegetable oil
2 cups spinach, washed and spun dry
1 small carrot, chopped
½ cup diced green beans
¼ cup sliced green onions
1 small jalapeño, seeded and finely chopped

Mix together the hoisin sauce, soy sauce, sesame oil, and garlic. Cut the steak in half lengthwise, and then cut it crosswise into inch-wide strips. Put the meat and the hoisin mixture into a nonreactive container and marinate, covered, in the refrigerator overnight.

Remove the meat from the marinade, reserving the marinade. Put the oil into a large skillet or wok set over high heat. When the oil begins to shimmer, stir-fry the bison, working in batches so as not to crowd the pan. Transfer the cooked pieces to a plate. Once the meat is cooked, add the spinach, carrot, green beans, and green onions and stir-fry to cook until just tender. Return the meat to the skillet, add some of the marinade, and bring it to a boil. Serve the meat and vegetables right away over barley, farro, or pasta.

Heartland Cheese Steak Sandwiches

Serves 2

Though Philly lays claim to these sandwiches, the truth is that the best ingredients come from the Heartland. Use great bread, a good-sized bone-in strip steak, and a solid Colby cheese (sorry, the traditional provolone will not do).

2 sturdy hoagie buns or 1 small baguette
1 tablespoon sunflower oil
1 (9- to 12-ounce) strip steak, about 1 inch thick
Coarse salt and freshly ground pepper
2 red or green bell peppers, cored, seeded, and thinly sliced
1 medium onion, thinly sliced
2 cloves garlic, sliced
2 ounces Colby cheese, thinly sliced

Preheat the broiler to high. Cut the bread in half lengthwise, and toast until golden, about 5 minutes. Set the bread aside.

In a large, heavy frying pan set over medium-high heat, warm the oil until it begins to shimmer, about 3 minutes. Season one side of the steak generously with salt. Using tongs, place the steak in the pan, salted-side down. Sear the steak without moving it for about 2 minutes. Season the top of the steak with salt, turn it, and sear for 2 more minutes. Transfer to a platter, and season both sides with pepper. Cover the meat loosely with aluminum foil.

Reduce the heat to medium, add the pepper and onion, and cook, stirring occasionally, until tender, about 5 minutes. Add the garlic, and cook another minute. Cover the pan, and remove it from the heat.

Cut the meat away from the bone; then cut it across the grain into slices about ⅛ inch thick, trimming away any excess fat. Return the steak and any juices on the platter to the pan, and season with salt and freshly ground pepper. Separate the mixture into 2 loose piles and divide the cheese between them, draping it across the top. Set the pan over very low heat, cover, and cook until the cheese has melted, about 1 to 2 minutes.

Place the bottom half of the bread on a plate. Using a wide spatula, carefully transfer the beef and then top with the other piece of bread. Serve right away.

Heartland Brisket

Serves 6

Make this in winter, when those hardy cattle and bison ranchers brave the ice and snow to get to the markets. The upside of our subzero months is that the farmers can display their wares on tables without worrying about them spoiling. This warming, classic pot roast tastes best made ahead so the meat's flavors intensify over time in the rich braising juices. To serve, simply warm the meat up in its juices. Leftovers piled on crusty rolls make great sandwiches.

¼ cup all-purpose flour
2 teaspoons sweet paprika
Coarse salt and freshly ground pepper
3 pounds beef brisket, trimmed of excess fat
2 tablespoons sunflower oil or vegetable oil
1 large onion, diced
3 slices bacon, cut into ½-inch strips
3 carrots, diced
1 small celeriac, diced
5 cloves garlic, smashed
5 sage leaves
3 sprigs rosemary
10 sprigs parsley
1 bay leaf
3 cups beer

On a large plate, stir together the flour, paprika, and a sprinkling of salt and pepper. Dredge the brisket in the flour, shaking off any excess.

Preheat the oven to 300 degrees.

In a large Dutch oven or a heavy ovenproof pot, heat the oil over medium and sauté the onion and bacon until the onion is soft, about 3 to 4 minutes. Increase the heat and brown the brisket, turning it until it is very brown on all sides, about 10 minutes. Remove the meat and set it aside.

Add the carrots, celeriac, garlic, sage, rosemary, parsley, bay leaf, and beer, scraping all the browned bits from the bottom of the pan. Bring to a low boil. Return the brisket to the pot, place the pot in the oven, and cook, turning the meat every 40 minutes, until it is fork-tender, about 4 to 5 hours. Transfer the brisket to a plate.

Taste the sauce, and adjust the seasoning. To serve, slice the brisket and pour some of the pan juices over the meat.

Pork

Pork, good pork from heirloom breeds, raised outside in the clean fresh air, is the most delicious, voluptuous meat of all. Maybe it's the fat and the way the skin crisps to a crackling crunch. Find this kind of pork from the farmers at market. It's well worth the trip.

GLORIOUS FAT!

A little fat goes a long way to add flavor and succulence to roasts and sautés. It's OK to trim a pork roast, but leave some of fat on a standing rib roast or a pork butt. This helps keep the meat stay tender and juicy in a hot, dry oven. Marbling refers to the little pockets of fat within a cut that help baste the meat internally and turn it succulent and flavorful. The real dietary fat culprits are fast foods—deep-fried snacks, processed meats, and sweets—not grilled T-bone steaks or pan-seared pork chops.

COOK'S NOTE

Heirloom hog breeds—Berkshire, Duroc, Red Wattle—are smaller animals, with more fat and thus more flavor. Along with better-tasting meat, the market farmers may also sell fresh lard. It's terrific for frying potatoes or making pie dough.

Grilled Pork Chops with Basil and Plums

Serves 4

Sweet plums caramelized quickly on the grill are a perfect complement to pork.

4 bone-in pork loin chops
Olive oil or sunflower oil
Coarse salt and freshly ground pepper
4 plums, quartered and pitted
2 tablespoons maple syrup
1 tablespoon apple cider vinegar
2 tablespoons chopped basil

Bring the chops to room temperature. Brush the chops with oil, and season them with salt and pepper.

In a bowl, toss together the plums, maple syrup, and 2 teaspoons of oil. Season with salt and pepper.

Prepare a charcoal or gas grill for medium-high heat. Place the chops on the grill rack over the hottest part of the fire, and sear both sides until golden, about 2 minutes per side. Move the chops to a cooler part of the grill, and cook until the pork is firm, about 3 to 4 minutes per side. An instant-read thermometer should show 145 degrees. Place the plums on the grill and sear until golden, about 20 to 30 seconds per side. Transfer the chops and the plums to a platter, and drizzle them with a little vinegar. Garnish with the basil.

Pork Belly Braised with Onions

Serves 4 to 6

Pork belly, aka fresh bacon, is the darling of restaurant chefs and no wonder. It's a deliciously rich, yielding, tender meat with a fabulously crisp skin. The farmers at markets are a great source of pastured pork belly (pork belly is not readily available in most grocery stores). Serve this over polenta (page 234) or cooked cranberry or white beans (page 68) for a satisfying Heartland meal.

1 tablespoon sunflower oil
Coarse salt and freshly ground pepper
2 pounds pork belly with skin
2 onions, sliced
4 cloves garlic, smashed
1 cup white wine
1 cup vegetable stock or chicken stock (page 264)
¼ cup chopped parsley

Preheat the oven to 350 degrees.

Heat the oil in a large ovenproof skillet over medium until it shimmers. Season the pork with salt and pepper, and sear it, fat-side down, until it's very brown, about 15 minutes. Transfer the pork to a plate.

Pour off all but 1 tablespoon of the fat, and add the onions and garlic. Cook, stirring, until they become tender and golden, about 15 minutes. Return the pork to the pan, fat-side up, and add the wine. Bring the liquid to a simmer, transfer the skillet to the oven, and cook, uncovered, for about 1 hour. Add a cup of stock and continue cooking until the pork is fork-tender, another hour.

Remove the pan from the oven, and allow the pork to cool in the pan. Once it is cool enough to handle, remove the pork from the braising liquid. Gently lift off and discard the skin. Score the fat on the pork, and then cut the pork into 4 or 6 equal-sized pieces.

Increase the oven temperature to 400 degrees. Strain the braising liquid through a fine-mesh strainer, and discard the solids. Return the liquid to the skillet, bring it to a simmer, and strain off the fat. Put the pork fat-side up in the skillet. Put the skillet in the oven, and cook until the pork is heated through and the fat is browned, about 20 to 30 minutes. Serve the pork with its juices over polenta, beans, or rice.

Pork Roast with Fennel and Pears

Serves 4 to 6

Porketta, the Iron Range favorite, gets a new twist from fresh fennel and sweet pears. Come January, make this with dried apricots; when spring arrives, use lemons to give it a lift.

3- to 4-pound pork butt, well trimmed
5 cloves garlic, slivered
1 large fennel bulb, trimmed and very coarsely chopped (about 1 ½ cups)
4 shallots, minced
3 ripe pears, peeled, cored, and cut into large dice
¼ cup dry sherry or dark beer
½ cup chicken stock (page 264)
1 tablespoon crushed fennel seeds
2 teaspoons coarse salt
Freshly ground pepper

Preheat the oven to 350 degrees.

Poke the meat all over with a thin-bladed knife and insert the garlic slivers into the holes. Put the fennel, shallots, pears, sherry, and stock into a large casserole or small roasting pan, and toss to combine. Put the pork in the pan, and pat the fennel seeds over the pork. Sprinkle with the salt and pepper. Cover with a lid or foil, and cook the pork until it's easily pierced with a sharp knife and its juices run clear, about 4 hours.

Allow the roast to rest in the pan for about 5 minutes before carving. Serve with fennel, pears, and pan juices spooned over the top.

Sweet and Salty Oven-Crisped Spareribs

Serves 6 to 8

The meat on these ribs is so tender it melts right off the bone. Look for lemon grass at the farmers market. If it's not available, substitute lemon zest.

2 stalks lemon grass, inner parts only, finely chopped,
    or 2 teaspoons grated lemon rind
2 tablespoons grated ginger
5 cloves garlic, minced
½ cup honey
⅓ cup soy sauce
3 tablespoons sunflower oil
2 large lemons
Salt and freshly ground pepper
2 racks (about 6 pounds) pork spareribs
¼ cup chopped basil
2 tablespoons chopped cilantro

In a large roasting pan or baking dish, whisk together the lemongrass, ginger, garlic, honey, soy sauce, oil, and the juice of 1 lemon. Whisk in a little salt and pepper. Place the ribs in the pan, and turn to coat, rubbing the marinade into the nooks and crannies. Cover, and refrigerate overnight.

Before cooking, bring the meat to room temperature. Preheat the oven to 250 degrees. Line two baking sheets with aluminum foil or parchment paper, and set a wire rack in each pan. Put the ribs on the racks, meat-side up, and spoon the remaining marinade over the meat. Cook the ribs until they are very tender when poked with a fork, about 3 ½ to 4 hours. Remove the pans from the oven.

To brown the ribs, place the oven rack about 4 inches from the heat source and preheat the broiler to high. Broil until the fat on the ribs starts to sizzle and crisp, about 3 to 5 minutes. Remove, and allow to cool for about 5 minutes before cutting between the ribs to separate them.

Quarter the remaining lemon, and squeeze the juice over the ribs. Serve garnished with basil and cilantro.

Lamb

Lamb is the one meat that unites all cultures: nearly everyone in the world who eats meat eats lamb. The quality—that is, the tenderness and flavor—of lamb is determined by the animal's age rather than by the amount of marbling.

COOK'S NOTE

Baby lamb is slaughtered at 10 weeks, when the lamb weighs less than 20 pounds. Spring lamb refers to those lambs weighing 20 to 40 pounds. The meat from young lamb is pale pink and mild; as lamb ages, its flavor becomes stronger and more distinct. The grass-fed lamb sold at our farmers markets is far healthier and tastier than conventionally raised lamb.

Quick Ideas

Greek Lamb Pitas: Leftover lamb roast and lamb chops are delicious when thinly sliced and stuffed into pitas with yogurt, fresh oregano, basil, and chopped cucumbers.

Lamb Curry: Use leftover or ground lamb in your favorite curry recipe. Serve over rice with yogurt and chopped fresh cilantro.

Butterflied Leg of Lamb with Fresh Mint Marinade

Serves 6

Use this spicy-cool marinade for lamb brochettes and lamb chops too. It's best if the lamb is marinated in the refrigerator overnight and then brought to room temperature before cooking.

1 cup plus 2 tablespoons chopped mint leaves
3 cloves garlic, minced
2 tablespoons ground coriander
2 teaspoons paprika
2 teaspoons ground cumin
2 teaspoons ground pepper
1 teaspoon cayenne
¼ cup sunflower oil
¼ cup fresh lemon juice
1 (4-pound) leg of lamb, boned and butterflied
Coarse salt

In a nonreactive container, whisk together 1 cup of mint, garlic, coriander, paprika, cumin, pepper, cayenne, sunflower oil, and lemon juice. Rub the marinade over the meat, cover, and marinate for 2 hours at room temperature or in the refrigerator overnight.

Before cooking, bring the lamb to room temperature. Prepare a gas or charcoal grill or preheat the broiler to high. Remove the lamb from the marinade, and sprinkle it with salt. Grill or broil, turning once, until the meat thermometer registers 120 degrees (for rare), about 10 to 15 minutes per side. For medium-well done, the thermometer should read 145 degrees. Allow it to rest for about 10 to 15 minutes before carving. Serve garnished with additional chopped mint.

Lamb Chops with Gremolata

Serves 4 to 6

8 single-rib lamb chops, about 2 ½ ounces each
Extra-virgin olive oil
2 teaspoons minced rosemary
Salt and freshly ground pepper
Grated zest of 1 lemon
1 clove garlic, crushed
2 tablespoons minced mint
Coarse salt

Pat the chops dry and rub them with olive oil; then rub in the fresh rosemary and sprinkle them with salt and pepper.

Prepare a charcoal or gas grill for medium-high heat. Place the chops on the grill rack over the hottest part of the fire, and sear both sides until golden, about 2 minutes per side. Move the chops to a cooler part of the grill, and cook until the lamb is firm, about 3 to 4 minutes per side. An instant-read thermometer should register 145 degrees for medium-well done.

In a small bowl, toss together the lemon zest, garlic, and mint. Sprinkle this on the lamb chops as they come from the grill. Drizzle them with a little more olive oil and salt and pepper before serving.

Lamb Burgers with Tzatziki

Serves 4

Tzatziki is a tangy Greek yogurt sauce that works beautifully with lamb patties. To serve, place these in slit pita bread or on top of sliced, lightly toasted olive bread for an open-faced sandwich.

LAMB BURGERS:

1 ¼ pounds coarsely ground lamb
2 tablespoons chopped oregano
1 tablespoon cumin
2 cloves garlic, finely chopped
Salt and freshly cracked pepper
Olive oil

TZATZIKI:

2 cups plain Greek-style yogurt or strained whole-milk yogurt
2 tablespoons lemon juice
½ cup diced cucumber
1 tablespoon minced dill
1 clove garlic, minced

In a large bowl, gently work together the lamb, oregano, cumin, and garlic. Lightly season the meat with salt and pepper.

With a light hand, form 4 loosely packed patties, and then gently flatten them to about ³/₄ inch thick. Brush the patties with some olive oil.

In a small bowl, whisk together the yogurt, lemon juice, cucumber, dill, and garlic.

Prepare a charcoal or gas grill for medium-high heat, or preheat a cast-iron skillet over medium-high heat and film it with olive oil. Place the burgers on the grill or in the skillet, and cook until nicely seared on both sides, about 3 minutes per side. Continue cooking, brushing with a little more oil if grilling, until the burgers are medium-rare or an instant-read thermometer registers 140 degrees.

Serve topped with the tzatziki in sliced pita bread, on a slice of olive bread, or a hamburger bun.

Poultry

CHICKEN, TURKEY, AND DUCK

Farmers markets are a great source for free-range poultry, duck, and goose. Many farmers raise heritage breeds. They are slaughtered later than conventionally raised poultry, and are thus heavier and meatier than those found in supermarkets.

COOK'S NOTE

Heritage breeds are leaner and have more muscle than conventionally raised birds. Use low heat, and baste frequently. Lean birds, such as quail or pheasant, are best barded with bacon, pancetta, or prosciutto.

Unlike commercially raised chickens, which are bred to have big breasts and small thighs, you'll find that free-range chickens have more dark meat and less white meat. These chickens tend to be just a little tougher than conventional chickens, so cook them slowly with low heat. Their flavor is far superior.

Save the bones for stock. Collect the bones of cooked chicken and store them in bags in the freezer. When you have a potful, put them in a large saucepan, cover them with water, add a carrot, an onion, and herbs, and simmer on low for an hour to make a terrific stock.

Farmer's Roast Chicken

Serves 4 to 6

A good roasted chicken will never let you down. The best roasters are a little older than those young hens sold in supermarkets as fryers. This recipe yields enough for a fine Sunday dinner with leftovers to see you through the week.

1 (4-pound) roasting chicken
2 lemons
Salt and freshly ground pepper
1 head garlic, cloves peeled and smashed
¼ cup unsalted butter, softened
1 cup mixed herbs (rosemary, thyme, parsley), coarsely chopped
½ cup white wine

Preheat the oven to 450 degrees. Rinse the chicken inside and out in cold water, and pat it dry. Cut the lemons in half, and squeeze the juice over the chicken inside and out. Season the chicken with salt and pepper inside and out, and then put the lemon halves and garlic cloves inside the chicken.

Loosen the breast skin at the rear of the chicken and very gently work your fingers under the skin; then spread some of the butter and half of the herb mixture under the chicken's skin. Rub the rest of the butter over the outside of the chicken, sprinkle some of the herb mix over that, and put the rest of the herbs inside the chicken's cavity. Set the chicken on a rack in a roasting pan, and roast for about 20 minutes. Reduce the heat to 350 degrees, and continue roasting until the juices in the thigh run clear when the chicken is poked with a sharp knife (a meat thermometer should register 170 degrees for dark meat, 160 degrees for white meat), about 55 to 65 minutes.

Transfer the chicken to a platter to rest for about 10 to 15 minutes before serving. Degrease the pan juices, set the pan over medium-high heat, and simmer to reduce the juices by half. Add the wine, and continue simmering until the juices have further reduced and will lightly coat a spoon.

Carve the chicken and serve it with the pan juices.

Chicken Sauté with Asparagus, Cherry Tomatoes, and Lemon

Serves 4

This is a quick, bright dish that is great served over noodles or farro.

4 medium-sized skinless chicken breasts, cut into ¾-inch chunks
Salt and freshly ground pepper
Sunflower oil
16 cherry tomatoes, halved
12 asparagus spears, trimmed, halved lengthwise, and cut into 2-inch pieces
6 cloves garlic, sliced
½ cup chicken stock (page 264)
¼ cup lemon juice
3 tablespoons unsalted butter
2 tablespoons chopped basil
2 tablespoons chopped parsley

Season the chicken with salt and pepper. Film a large skillet with some oil, and set it over high heat. Add the tomatoes and asparagus, and cook, stirring, until the tomatoes have softened and the asparagus begins to brown, about 2 to 3 minutes. Transfer to a medium bowl.

Heat a little more oil in the skillet, and add the chicken, turning to sear it on all sides, about 5 to 8 minutes. Add the chicken to the bowl with the vegetables.

Reduce the heat to low. Add a little more oil and then the garlic, and cook, stirring, until it is golden, about 1 minute. Add the stock and the lemon juice, stirring to scrape up any browned bits that cling to the bottom of the pan. Simmer until the liquid is reduced by half. Swirl in the butter, and then return the chicken and vegetables to the skillet to warm through. Season the sauté with salt and pepper, and toss in the basil and parsley.

Holiday Turkey with Cranberry Sage Butter

Serves 8 to 10

The best turkeys at the market are the smallest. If you're feeding a crowd, two birds in the oven are better than a great big one. In this recipe, cranberry sage butter is tucked under the skin to baste the turkey while it roasts and then slathered over the turkey just before it comes out of the oven. Be sure to save some to serve on the side.

1 small turkey, about 8 to 12 pounds
Salt and freshly ground pepper
½ cup fresh cranberries
¼ cup apple cider
1 cup unsalted butter
2 tablespoons sage
1 shallot, minced
4 strips good-quality bacon

Preheat the oven to 375 degrees. Rinse the turkey inside and out, and pat it dry. Season it inside and out with salt and freshly ground pepper.

In a small saucepan set over medium-low heat, cook the cranberries in the cider until they pop. Turn the mixture into a food processor fitted with a steel blade, add the butter, sage, and shallot, and process until combined.

Loosen the breast skin at the rear of the turkey and work your fingers under the skin; then work some of the butter mixture up under the skin and along the breast. Rub more of

the butter over the outside of the bird, saving some to finish the turkey later. Drape the bacon over the turkey breast. Set the turkey on a roasting rack in a roasting pan, and roast, basting frequently with the pan juices and adding more cranberry-sage butter as needed. Continue roasting until an instant-read thermometer registers 170 degrees for dark meat, 160 degrees for white meat, about 1 ½ to 2 ½ hours, depending on the size of your turkey. About 5 minutes before pulling the turkey from the oven, brush it all over with the remaining cranberry sage butter. Allow the turkey to rest about 20 minutes before carving.

Old-Fashioned Roast Duck
with Rosemary Honey Glaze

Serves 4

If you are not a hunter (and don't know one), find wonderful duck at the farmers market. The trick to getting moist duck meat and crisp skin is to prick the skin as the duck roasts. This releases the fat that bastes the duck as it cooks.

2 large (4- to 5-pound) ducks
Coarse salt and freshly ground pepper
1 large shallot, chopped
½ cup apple cider
¼ cup cider vinegar
2 sprigs rosemary
¼ cup honey
1 large tart apple, peeled, cored, and thinly sliced

Preheat the oven to 500 degrees.

Remove the giblets from the duck cavities and reserve them for another use. Trim off the wing tips and any neck fat. Rinse the ducks and pat them dry. Rub the meat inside and out with coarse salt and ground pepper. Lightly prick the skin all over with a fork, being careful not to pierce the flesh. Set the ducks on a rack in a large roasting pan.

Roast the ducks for 20 minutes. Reduce the heat to 350 degrees, and lightly prick the ducks again. Roast until the skin is golden brown and an instant-read thermometer inserted into the thickest part of the thigh registers 170 degrees (or until the juices are rosy to yellow), about 55 to 65 minutes longer, depending on the size of the ducks. Transfer the ducks to a carving board, and let them rest for 15 to 30 minutes before carving.

While the ducks are resting, make the sauce. Pour all but 1 tablespoon of the duck fat from the roasting pan, and place the pan on the stovetop over medium heat. Add the shallot, and sauté until it is translucent, about 2 to 3 minutes. Raise the heat to high, add the cider, vinegar, and rosemary sprigs, and deglaze the pan, scraping up any browned bits from the bottom. Cook until the liquid is reduced by half, about 3 to 5 minutes. Reduce the heat to low, whisk in the honey, and add the apple slices. Taste, and adjust the sauce. Remove the rosemary sprigs.

Carve each duck into thigh-leg and boneless breast portions and arrange them on a warmed serving platter with the apple slices. Drizzle with the sauce, and put the remaining sauce in a warmed bowl to pass at the table.

EGGS

The early bird gets the eggs at the St. Paul Farmers Market. Farmers sell out quickly, and no wonder. Fresh eggs sport the brightest yolks and the most distinctly eggy flavor. They whip up into lofty meringues and make the creamiest custards. Duck eggs are bigger and even richer-tasting than chicken's eggs and make a luxurious golden scramble or omelet.

COOK'S NOTE

When substituting duck eggs for chicken eggs, count on using 1 duck egg for every 2 large chicken eggs.

Quick Ideas

Deviled Eggs: Boil eggs for about 17 minutes in enough water to cover them. Cool the eggs, peel and halve them, and scoop out the yolks. Mix the yolks with good mayonnaise, chopped chives, and a little paprika, and then use it to stuff the whites. Serve cold.

Crustless Quiche: Use your favorite quiche recipe for the filling, but instead of making a crust, generously butter or grease a pie pan, and then dust it with dried bread crumbs.

Asparagus, Cheddar, and Potato Frittata

Serves 4

A frittata is a flat Spanish omelet, served in wedges at room temperature (never warm). This recipe calls for spring vegetables, but please do vary the ingredients to use what's in season.

8 large eggs
3 tablespoons chopped fresh parsley
Salt and freshly ground pepper
Generous pinch of crushed red pepper
2 tablespoons vegetable oil or olive oil
1 Yukon Gold potato, scrubbed and cut into ½-inch dice
1 medium yellow onion, thinly sliced
½ pound medium-thick asparagus, trimmed and cut into 1-inch pieces
3 cloves garlic, minced
6 ounces cheddar, grated

In a medium bowl, whisk together the eggs, parsley, salt, pepper, and crushed red pepper.

Heat the oil in an ovenproof 10-inch skillet over medium-high heat. Add the potato and a sprinkle of salt, and cook, stirring, until the potato is browned on all sides, about 7 to 8 minutes. Transfer to a bowl.

Reduce the heat, add the onion, and cook until it softens and begins to brown, about 5 minutes. Stir in the asparagus, garlic, and a little salt and pepper. Cook until the asparagus is bright green and tender-crisp, 3 to 4 minutes.

Position an oven rack 6 inches from the broiler and preheat the broiler to high.

Lower the heat under the pan, and add the eggs and the potatoes, stirring until the ingredients are combined, 10 to 15 seconds. Add the cheddar, and stir until it's distributed. Cook without stirring until the eggs have nearly set, 10 to 12 minutes. The center may still be loose, but the sides should be set.

Transfer the skillet to the oven, and cook under the broiler until the eggs have set completely and the top of the frittata is golden, 3 to 5 minutes. Let the frittata rest for 5 minutes before transferring it to a cutting board. Cut the frittata into 4 wedges and serve.

Meringue Shell

Makes one 9-inch shell

This light, crisp meringue shell is great filled with lemon curd made with the leftover yolks (see recipe below) and topped with plenty of berries and whipped cream.

¼ teaspoon salt
1 cup sugar
1 tablespoon cornstarch
4 egg whites, at room temperature
1 teaspoon vanilla
½ teaspoon lemon juice

Preheat the oven to 225 degrees. Line a cookie sheet with parchment paper.

Mix together the salt, sugar, and cornstarch in a small bowl. In a large bowl, beat the egg whites until soft peaks form. Gradually add the sugar mixture, 1 tablespoon at a time, beating well after each addition. Beat in the vanilla and the lemon juice.

Mound the meringue onto the prepared cookie sheet, and use a rubber spatula to spread it into a 9- or 10-inch circle. Bake until lightly browned and crisp, about 1 hour. Allow to cool before filling.

Lemon Curd

Makes about 1 cup

This makes delicious use of the egg yolks left over from making meringues.

Grated zest of 2 lemons
½ cup lemon juice
4 egg yolks
1 cup sugar
Pinch of salt
2 tablespoons unsalted butter

In a medium saucepan, beat together the lemon zest, lemon juice, egg yolks, sugar, and salt. Cook over low heat, stirring constantly, until the mixture becomes thick and translucent, about 5 to 7 minutes. It should coat the back of a spoon. Remove from the stove, and strain through a fine-mesh strainer into a separate bowl. Stir in the butter until it's melted.

Use the lemon curd to fill the meringue shell, or store it, covered, in the refrigerator for up to 1 week.

Fish

Especially along the Lake Superior shores, farmers markets feature local whitefish and lake trout. In the Twin Cities, trout, perch, and tilapia come from nearby organic fish farms.

Whole Grilled Trout with Lemon Thyme Marinade

Serves 4

This light and tangy marinade works wonderfully with trout and salmon, but don't let the fish marinate long because the lemon juice will make its flesh too soft.

½ cup lemon juice
3 cloves garlic, minced
2 tablespoons thyme leaves
½ cup sunflower oil or vegetable oil
4 small (8- to 10-inch) trout, cleaned with heads left on
Salt and freshly ground pepper
4 scallions, trimmed
¼ cup chopped parsley
Lemon wedges

In a small bowl, whisk together the lemon juice, garlic, thyme, and oil. Rinse the trout and pat them dry. Generously salt and pepper the cavity of each fish and put 1 scallion in each cavity. Place the trout in a large dish, pour the marinade over them, and allow them to stand for about 10 minutes at room temperature.

Preheat the grill to medium-high. Remove the trout from the marinade, and place them on the grill. Cook the trout, brushing them liberally with the marinade, until they are opaque and flake easily, about 4 to 5 minutes per side. Serve garnished with chopped parsley and lemon wedges.

Smoked Trout or Whitefish Pâté

Makes about 1½ cups

Serve this in endive spears or on cucumber rounds. It's also great spread on thick slices of rye bread and topped with chopped onions for an open-face sandwich.

3 ounces smoked trout or whitefish, skinned and boned
1 cup soft cream cheese
2 tablespoons lemon juice
Several dashes Tabasco sauce
Milk as needed
1 tablespoon snipped chives

Put the fish, the cream cheese, the lemon juice, and the Tabasco sauce into a food processor fitted with a steel blade. Pulse until the mixture is smooth. Thin with milk if necessary. Fold in the chives.

Market Essentials

Market Essentials

Stock the pantry with these essentials, and keep these quick go-to recipes for vinaigrettes and sauces on hand.

Basic Mayonnaise

Makes ½ cup

1 large egg yolk
1 tablespoon lemon juice
½ teaspoon Dijon mustard
¼ teaspoon salt
½ cup sunflower oil

In a large bowl, whisk together the egg yolk, lemon juice, mustard, and salt. Pour in the oil in a slow, steady stream, whisking constantly until it is incorporated. Serve immediately, or refrigerate in a covered container for up to 3 days.

Essential Vinaigrette

Makes 1 cup

Make up a large batch of this vinaigrette in advance to have on hand; then add the chopped fresh herbs right before using. This will ensure that it tastes fresh.

⅓ cup apple cider vinegar
1 tablespoon minced shallot
Salt and freshly ground pepper
¾ cup sunflower oil or olive oil
2 tablespoons chopped herbs (tarragon, basil, thyme, rosemary, parsley, alone or in combination)

In a medium bowl, whisk together the vinegar, shallot, salt, and pepper, and then add the oil, whisking it in slowly. Whisk in the herbs right before using.

Maple Mustard Vinaigrette

Makes about 1 ½ cups

Use this to dress grain salads and to glaze grilled chicken or fish.

¼ cup apple cider vinegar
1 small shallot, chopped
2 tablespoons coarse Dijon mustard
¼ cup maple syrup
¾ cup sunflower oil

In a small bowl, whisk together the vinegar, shallot, mustard, and maple syrup. While whisking, add the oil in a slow, steady stream.

Honey Mustard Basting Sauce

Makes ¾ cup

This makes a lovely basting sauce for grilled pork or chicken.

½ cup maple syrup
¼ cup Dijon mustard
2 tablespoons apple cider vinegar

Simply combine the maple syrup, mustard, and vinegar in a bowl, and whisk to combine.

Speedy Vegetable Stock

Makes 2 quarts

This is the go-to stock. It's easy, it's fast, and it's lighter than chicken stock. Use just about any vegetables you have on hand, except cabbage, cauliflower, broccoli, and kale, as they will take over the pot.

4 carrots, cut into chunks
2 medium onions, unpeeled and quartered
1 stalk celery or 1 small celeriac, cut into chunks
4 cloves garlic
30 stems parsley
Salt and freshly ground pepper

Put all the ingredients in a big pot with water to cover by about 1 inch. Bring the water to a boil, and then reduce the heat so the liquid bubbles slowly. Cook until the vegetables are tender, about 30 minutes. Strain out the vegetables, and season to taste with additional salt and pepper.

Essential Chicken Stock

Makes about 1 gallon

While using a whole chicken may sound a bit extravagant, doing so yields a flavorful broth, especially if you use a farmers market chicken. After it's been simmering for about an hour, remove the chicken and take out the breasts to use in salads, soups, or stews; return the rest of the chicken to the pot. Be sure not to cook this at a boil, as the stock will become cloudy and greasy. Remember to skim off the foam every so often.

This stock will keep about a week in the refrigerator and up to 2 weeks if you bring to a boil before using it. It will also freeze for up to 6 months. But if the stock smells off, discard it.

1 (3¼- to 4-pound) whole chicken
1 ½ gallons cold water, or more to cover
1 carrot
1 stalk celery with leaves
1 onion, peeled and halved
6 cloves garlic
1 bay leaf
2 sprigs thyme
5 sprigs parsley
1 teaspoon peppercorns
½ teaspoon coarse salt

Put the chicken and the water in a stockpot. Bring the water to a boil, and then immediately reduce the heat. Skim off the foam, and simmer on low for about 1 hour. Remove the chicken, and cut out the breasts to reserve for another use. Return the remaining chicken parts to the stock, and continue simmering for another 3 to 4 hours. Skim the stock frequently.

When the stock is done, allow it to cool to room temperature and then chill it. Remove the layer of fat, and then strain out the remaining chicken, vegetables, and herbs before using.

Essential Pastry Crust

Makes one 10-inch pie or tart crust

This is a buttery rich crust, delicious for fruit pies, pastries, and tarts. Cut the sugar and use it for meat pies and quiche.

1 ½ cups all-purpose flour
2 tablespoons sugar (omit for savory pies)
Pinch of salt
½ cup cold unsalted butter, cut into pieces
3 to 4 tablespoons ice water

Sift the flour, sugar, and salt into a large bowl. Using a pastry cutter, two knives, or your fingertips, cut the butter into the flour until the mixture resembles small peas.

Sprinkle the water over the dough, and toss with a fork until the pastry comes together. Add more water if necessary, but be careful not to moisten the dough too much. Gather the pastry into a ball, and flatten it into a disk. Wrap it in plastic wrap or parchment paper, and chill for at least 1 hour before rolling out the dough.

Spirited Whipped Cream

Makes 2 cups

Whip your favorite dessert wine or liquor into cream to top pies and cakes.

1 cup heavy cream
2 tablespoons sugar
¼ cup applejack or your favorite liquor

In a medium bowl, whip the cream and sugar until stiff peaks form. Fold in the liquor.

Toasting Nuts

Toasting nuts intensifies their flavors and is worth the little extra time it takes to do. Rely on your nose when toasting nuts. As soon as they begin to smell nutty, they are ready to be pulled out of the oven.

To toast nuts, spread the nuts out on a baking sheet, and roast in a 350-degree oven for 3 to 5 minutes, or until they become lightly browned.

Hazelnuts have a fine, papery skin that should be removed after roasting. Put the nuts in a damp towel, fold it over the nuts, and rub. The skins will flake off.

Farmers Market Menus

LATE SPRING LUNCH

When the asparagus are in, don't wait—get several bundles and enjoy them right away!

Herb Popovers (page 136)
Smoked Trout or Whitefish Pâté on Toasts (page 259)
Fresh Asparagus Soup (page 62)
Strawberries with Sabayon (page 48)

MIDSUMMER AT THE GRILL

Fire up the grill, and linger under the stars.

Chèvre Cheese Spread (page 222)
Lamb Chops with Gremolata (page 248)
Tuscan Farro Salad (page 227)
Radish, Cucumber, and Mint Salad (page 177)
Cherry Clafouti (page 23)

MARKET PICNIC

Rustle up a picnic basket, and head to the lake.

Quick Corn Toss (page 114)
Pasta Salad with Basic Pesto (page 135) and Cherry Tomatoes
Melon and Feta Salad in Mint Vinaigrette (page 35)
Currant Hazelnut Cake (page 30)

SUNDAY BREAKFAST UP NORTH

Sleep in! Here's a simple make-ahead menu.

Breakfast Blueberry Cobbler (page 20)
Asparagus, Cheddar, and Potato Frittata (page 256)
Poached Apricots (page 18)

MUSHROOM MANIA

When the lilacs are the size of mouse ears, the 'shrooms are in!

Mushrooms on Toast (page 151)
Mushroom and Tofu Miso Soup (page 152)
Wild Mushrooms with Barley (page 154)
Sunchokes and Baby Lettuces in Tarragon Vinaigrette (page 192)
Rhubarb Pandowdy (page 46)

HARVEST FEAST

Celebrate the bounty with a big spread!

Apple Mint Salsa (page 14) with Chèvre
Arugula and Raspberry Salad in Raspberry Vinaigrette (page 43)
Gingered Pear and Winter Squash Soup (page 40)
Beets and Beet Greens, North African Style (page 76)
Roasted Fennel and Pears (page 125)
Sweet and Salty Oven-Crisped Spareribs (page 246)
Apple Oat Bundt Cake with Cider Brandy Glaze (page 16)

MARKET THANKSGIVING

The turkey, surrounded by brilliant flavors and color, is the centerpiece of this feast to celebrate our fall harvest.

Apple, Walnut, and Blue Cheese Salad (page 223)
Holiday Turkey with Cranberry Sage Butter (page 253)
Caramelized Brussels Sprouts (page 88)
Squash with Rosemary and Parmesan (page 187)
Mashed Potatoes (page 173)
Fresh Cranberry Ginger Salsa (page 28)
Honey, Oat, Flax, and Sunny Quick Bread (page 233)
Pear Galette (page 39)

WINTER SOLSTICE FEAST

A blazing fire glazes the windows, while outside a bounty of stars pricks the black velvet sky. Now is the time to snuggle in and take your time with this dinner.

Curried Parsnip Soup (page 161)
Spinach Lasagna with Feta and Walnuts (page 185)
Greek-Style Beet and Yogurt Salad (page 78)
Meringues with Lemon Curd (page 257)

Acknowledgments

....

It takes a market to write a cookbook.

Minnesota's Bounty: The Farmers Market Cookbook celebrates thirty years of glorious exchanges with growers, vendors, market managers, cooks, and chefs. Back home, I owe family and friends credit for bringing these pages to life. Kevin, my husband, is a deep source of encouragement, wit, and wisdom; our sons, Matt, Kip, and Tim, have tasted my creations and cheered me over these happy years.

Mette Nielsen's sumptuous photographs reflect her enthusiasm, culinary skills, and keen eye for beauty and grace.

I couldn't have asked for a better editor than Todd Orjala—avid gardener, savvy cook, trusted mentor. Pam Price, knowledgeable and passionate cook, skillfully copyedited with insight, humor, and care. Many thanks to Kristian Tvedten for his care and patience as he guided these pages into a book.

....

Index

Beth Dooley has covered the local food scene in the Northern Heartland for twenty-five years: she is a restaurant critic for *Mpls.St.Paul Magazine,* writes for the Taste section of the Minneapolis and St. Paul *Star Tribune,* and appears regularly on KARE-11 (NBC) television in the Twin Cities area. She is author of *The Northern Heartland Kitchen* and coauthor with Lucia Watson of *Savoring the Seasons of the Northern Heartland,* both published by the University of Minnesota Press. She lives in Minneapolis with her husband and three sons.

Also Published by the University of Minnesota Press

....

Cooking Up the Good Life: Creative Recipes for the Family Table
Jenny Breen and Susan Thurston

Turn Here Sweet Corn: Organic Farming Works
Atina Diffley

The Northern Heartland Kitchen
Beth Dooley

Savoring the Seasons of the Northern Heartland
Beth Dooley and Lucia Watson

The Swedish Table
Helene Henderson

The Spoonriver Cookbook
Brenda Langton and Margaret Stuart

....

Notes

Notes